I may not ride a motorcycle to the bottom of the world, but my soul comes alive when I hear about people smashing fear and following their dreams. This book will truly inspire you.

—Abigail Irene Fisher, traveler and speaker

Dirk knows what he's talking about; but more importantly how to communicate that effectively in a way that makes you feel like you've shared his experiences with him. It's an easy read that's hard to put down.

—Garrison Wynn, Motivational and Keynote Speaker

This is not the first book I've read on riding to Ushuaia, but it is probably the most enjoyable. Dirk writes about his experiences in an upbeat manner, taking each experience and each day in perspective. He includes travel tips while avoiding digging into the negatives. He has made the most of his trip without deadlines and without a lot of prior planning. He takes the time to meet people along the way, befriending many. He follows his front wheel and enjoys the ride.

—Muriel Farrington, Ambassador, BMW Motorcycles Of America

Leave Tomorrow is a fun, engaging, and thought-provoking read. If you are looking for a blend of humanity, culture, scary moments with a medicine man, military police, attempts at extortion, and unexpected challenges—along with insightful observations and humor, this book will definitely spark your imagination to "live your own movie." Let Leave Tomorrow get you in the game of creating your adventure. You will be glad you did.

—Steve Scott, business coach and author of Wings To Fly

Having encountered Dirk just after he was blown off his bike (twice) by the diabolical winds around Mt Fitzroy, and then again, unexpectedly, half way up a mountain at the true End of the World, I can only attest to his beautiful spirit and wandering soul that took him on his amazing, grown-up adventure. This inspiring and entertaining book of his epic journey from Texas to Tiera del Fuego, is just the tonic needed to get you up out of your chair and ready to "Leave Tomorrow."

—Julie Mundy, Guidebook Author and Travel Blogger, Australia

Dirk reminds us that true freedom and adventure are readily available for those crazy enough to seek it.

—Matt Ham, Author of *Redefine Rich* and co-founder of YouPrint

After knowing and working with Dirk for over 40 years I can easily say he's one of the most enjoyable productive good guys here on earth. Dirk makes every day an adventure whether he's working, playing, or exploring new personal frontiers. Many people talk about their dreams. Dirk is living his. Motivational!

—Greg Thurman, Entrepreneur and Mentor

If safety and predictability are your ultimate goals in life, then this book isn't for you. But if you want a road map to living a life that is large and meaningful, then take the ultimate ride with Leave Tomorrow. Dirk isn't a dreamer with his head in the clouds. He's the ultimate doer. He's unafraid to chase the sun into the horizon until he sees what makes it burn. Chased by banditos, bitten by mosquitoes, and a consuming too many South American burritos, Dirk's ride through South America is one part travel guide, one part life instruction manual, and one part can't-put-down adventure book.

—David Rupert, Writer. Encourager.

I had the pleasure to meet Dirk in 2014 when he was thinking about making the trip to South America. In my business I am blessed to meet many interesting and adventurous people. Dirk stands out as an impressive individual. You could not hope to meet a nicer or more humble man. Yet he has a quality that makes you step back and think, this is a unique and extraordinary person! I am proud to say that I sold Dirk the BMW R1200GSA he took on his adventures. It is an inspiration to read about his journey. This book makes me want to put my life in perspective and LEAVE TOMORROW on my own adventure!

—Sean MCafee, Woods Fun Center, BMW Motorcycle Dealer, Austin Texas

For everyone thinking of a new adventure, a new life, or even a new venture: DO IT.

—Jim Rogers, bestselling author of *Investment Biker* and *Street Smarts*

LEAVE TOMORROW

MY RIDE TO THE BOTTOM OF THE WORLD.

DIRK WEISIGER

Jan —
Live your Movie!
"Ride" your journey!

DIRK 2018

Leave Tomorrow

My Ride to the Bottom of the World.

Live Your Movie.

ISBN-13: 978-1977877130

ISBN-10: 1977877133

www.DirkWeisiger.com

See more photos and notes at www.DirkWeisiger.com/Chapters

CONTENTS

This book is dedicated to my two biggest fans: my son, Brian and daughter, Laura. You inspire me to stay young and embrace the future. I love you! (And I'm your biggest fan.)

ONE

ARE YOU CRAZY?

Someone told me there was a great restaurant called, Tierra del Fuego. So I jumped on the Iron Horse and rode to check it out.

They forgot to mention, or maybe I misunderstood, the restaurant was actually located at the very tip of South America. Well, I'm always in search of an excellent enchilada dinner, so I rode south.

THIS IS HOW I sometimes introduce tales of a journey that changed my life. No, I wasn't having a sudden midlife crisis. I've been in a midlife crisis since age eighteen. On this trip, and previous adventures, I didn't leave some "normal" life behind. I've always despised normal. I found myself in a season of life with freedom, flexibility—and hunger.

Part of me was searching for an elusive beach with a hammock between two palm trees. But a deeper part of me wanted adventure, connection, and the opportunity to explore what I was really made of.

"Must be nice to take off on a trip through Central and South America," many have said. Truth is, every one of us has more freedom than we realize.

SUNSETS

I GREW UP on a ranch in south Texas, and as I rode my horse, I'd often stare into the reddened sunset sky and wonder what was on the other side of the horizon.

Now I' know. Partially anyway. But I'm still searching for more. How about you?

At the age of eighteen, two buddies (Bo and John) and I left our friends and family in Texas and headed out to work on a ranch in Wyoming. There was even a write-up about our trip in the local paper. This wasn't the first time I heard the expression, "Are you crazy?" And it sure wasn't the last.

Honestly, the fascination of the old west and being a cowboy is more fascinating from afar. The experience was hard and lonely. My pay was $250 per month, which included room and board. We doctored and fed five thousand cattle on the LX Bar Ranch in Arvada, Wyoming.

I sharpened my skills as a rider and roper. Having grown up on a ranch in South Texas, I was a pretty good hand. It was all I knew.

I've worked with all sorts of savory characters— some running from the law and some that oughta. Most were good people, living their movie and walking out their journey. The traveling cowboy is a slice of Americana that's fading away.

I grew up a lot in those two years. I'll always cherish my first travel adventure, and I yearned for more.

Growing up, my parents often inquired about my mental health. *Are you crazy, Dirk?* They never knew what I'd try next. My ranch buddies were no different. But after two years working on ranches, my father asked me about my plans for the future. "Maybe try college," he suggested.

I took his suggestion.

THE DOOR-TO-DOOR BIBLE SALESMAN

AT AGE TWENTY-ONE, I needed a way to pay for college. My father told me about an opportunity selling Bibles door to door. My sister, who was in college, agreed to give Bible selling a try. Dad felt more comfortable letting her sell if I was there to watch over her.

I had nothing to lose but $250 a month and a herd of smelly cattle.

The publishing company representative said I could make $5,000 in just three months, and they would teach me how to be a winner. I was slow with math but figured rather quickly this could be the job for me.

Tossing my saddle in the back of my pickup, I figured I could head back to work at summer roundup in Wyoming if this new venture didn't work out. I drove my sister to Nashville to start our new lives.

The Southwestern Company sold books door to

door around the USA with a summertime sales force of college kids. It was straight commission.

I'd never been comfortable around college kids, and the job training didn't help. The training event was like a pep rally. I wasn't so sure about my decision until I heard a speech that changed my life.

On day three of the training week, my future sales manager told all the students about his decision to sell books. Someone had said to him, "Anybody can be a success in life, but when are you gonna start?"

Those words hit me like a kick from a horse. My thinking took a 180-degree turn, and I became serious about my new beginning. I was gonna start that day.

My sales manager, Greg Thurman, became my mentor—and still is, forty years later. I went on to be his top rookie salesman. My check at the end of the first summer totaled $4,300. I sold Bibles for four summers, put myself through college, and earned a degree that would've been a fantasy five years earlier. I crammed four years into five!

My journey had taken an unexpected turn—for the better.

LONG-TERM CARE

AFTER COLLEGE, I sold many different products—everything from phone systems, bank services, office space leases, to real estate magazine ads. And I spent a lot of time looking into the sunsets.

I was "between gigs" when my old friend Greg called.

"How would you like to sell lawn care, Dirk?"

"I've already got a lawn service," I answered.

"No, *long-term care*," he repeated.

He was starting a new sales division to sell long-term care insurance through banks. I said yes.

For the next twenty-seven years, I sold insurance products to help people pay for the high costs of living in a nursing home. My career provided a comfortable living and the opportunity for my children to attend college. My sister Amy continues to lead our company today.

A colleague asked me if I was crazy when I had the idea to incorporate trick roping into my sales presentations. I once spoke to an AARP group in a small town about long-term care.

We advertised in the local paper, and the ad read, "Dirk the Roping Cowboy" would be performing rope tricks, telling cowboy stories, and sharing about long-term care.

When I showed up at the venue, there was a line of people waiting around the corner! The clubhouse was packed with retirees who wanted to hear Will Rogers. I entertained for thirty minutes and spent five minutes mentioning insurance.

Twenty-one people bought a policy. Sometimes you've got to live your own movie and think outside the box. And love people. Care about people, and they will care about you.

INTO AFRICA

MY FRIENDS WONDERED about my judgment when, in 2005 and at the age of forty-eight, I decided to

5

travel to Africa and climb Mt. Kilimanjaro.

I even lugged my rope 19,346 feet to the summit and performed some rope tricks. I remember training for six months for the climb. My buddy Art told me, "You'll be fine till 14,000 feet above sea level, but after that, all bets are off."

I'd done everything I could to be ready and prepared. As we climbed the mountain, each step was more challenging. Five steps and I had to rest. I was following my guide, but I was tired and wanted to quit. I wasn't sure I could make it—or if I wanted to. But what I *did* know was I could take one more step.

Our guide would take a step, and I would concentrate on putting my step in his step. I knew if I put my step in his step, I'd make it to the top. A good metaphor for our need to depend on a higher power.

Friends, you can *want* to make a movie, you can pick a journey, and you can even leave tomorrow, but are you going to quit before you're almost there? Quitting is the worst kind of crazy.

Don't quit. Take one more step. Fight one more round.

DAD, I'M WORRIED ABOUT YOU

IN 2012, I was "homeless." Not really, but I'd decided to simplify my life. I kept simplifying until I sold my house. Then I hit the open road. On my first excursion, I headed to Canada for several weeks with just a tent and a cot.

My daughter confided, "Um, Dad. I'm worried about you... You're homeless."

"Stories of my demise have been greatly exaggerated," I explained to her.

I was recently divorced, and although I enjoyed the people aspect of my work, I wondered if there wasn't more to life than this hamster wheel.

Travel was my outlet. My medicine. The places I hadn't been were the places I wanted to go!

GO SOUTH

I REALLY GOT some questions and funny looks when I decided to ride my motorcycle from Texas to the tip of South America.

To be fair, there were a few reasons for my friends to be concerned.

I hadn't even ridden a motorcycle before 2012 and sure couldn't fix one if you put a gun to my head, which seemed to be a possible scenario for the journey I was planning.

I don't use a GPS, and some of my greatest adventures are the result of getting lost.

The only Spanish I knew was cafe con leche. And *extra queso*. Oh, and *cerveza*.

Many people who know me are surprised when they hear about my adventures because I'm just a regular guy. I'm no daredevil, but I love to explore new places. And I've never met a stranger. Even if we don't speak a common language, we share something even more powerful.

Solo travel is gratifying because you have to step out of your comfort zone. It forces you to face life with no backup plan, and having no plan makes you see life in a foreign place as it really is, not the tourist version. Sometimes, a change in perception is the stark reality of truth.

SOLD BY A BOOK

IN 2013, I read a book called *Investment Biker* by the legendary investor, Jim Rogers. His story of a twenty-two-month, fifty-two-country, motorcycle trek, inspired me to do something crazy.

But after two years, I still hadn't left.

So, I emailed Jim. I told him how he had inspired me to ride my motorcycle (the Iron Horse) from Texas to Ushuaia, Argentina, but I was having trouble starting. Did he have any advice?

I thought he'd provide route suggestions, ideas on where to stay, what kind of bike to use, and maybe share his favorite color.

His reply changed my life, and it consisted of just two words: "DO IT." Those words inspired me to leave tomorrow. So I did. Almost.

I quit procrastinating and started planning. The trip moved from an idea to action. It took me a couple of months to turn my company over to my sister. The same sister I drove to Nashville all those years ago. I told her I'd be back soon... maybe. I didn't know if the trek would take five months or five years. Or if I'd ever make it back.

But I knew I could start.

You see, I wrote this book to inspire you to live *your* movie.

LIFE HAPPENS IN SEASONS

YEAH, WHEN YOU watch TV news, the world looks pretty messed up. And maybe when you look in the mirror, life seems pretty messed up. But when you step, or ride, out of your comfort zone, the view changes. A lot.

We all make mistakes, and we all carry regrets. We all get stuck, but God doesn't want us to stay stuck. Yes, faith is important in life—and so is travel. You and I can see to the end of our street, but God sees around the bend. I'm a very common man, and I look to God for guidance and mercy.

This book isn't a Sunday School lesson, but might be a Monday-school lesson in pursuing your dreams.

Even if the traffic lights aren't all green, and they never are, leave tomorrow.

You'll face obstacles, but you'll figure it out along the way. That's the joy of adventure. You can't plan a life, but you can plan a change or a trek.

What's your adventure? This book is about my journey, but yours might be beginning a new career, starting a family, traveling around the world, or stepping across the street.

You'll become a better storyteller, and more importantly, a better listener.

Do you have a hunger for adventure but don't know where to start? Tag along with me in my journey. I believe my stories will inspire you to:

- live your own movie,
- walk your own Journey,
- and leave tomorrow.

RETURN TO WIMBERLEY—Dirk Weisiger and John Hunt have returned to Wimberley after a seven-month tour of the Western states. They're pictured with their faithful conveyance and companion throughout the trip, the pick-up truck that saw them safely through their journies and back to Wimberley. Please see story in ABOUT TOWN.

Two

TRAINING WHEELS IN MEXICO

AS WE NEARED Laredo, Texas, it was eerily quiet and hot.

December 26, 2015, turned out to be Summer-like and dusty. We veered to the left from I-35 and headed to a lesser-used border crossing south of Laredo. I was following J.D., a fellow rider from Austin, who I met when I bought my used BMW R1200GSA Adventure Bike. He was the previous owner and knew the motorcycle better than I did.

J.D. has ridden in Mexico every year for the past twenty-plus years and knows the country like the back of his hand. The next two weeks would be my personal crash-course in cross-country riding.

I knew nothing, but I had the courage to try.

As we approached the border, my anxiety rose while keeping an eye out for the drug cartel. My family and friends were concerned for my safety, but J.D. was as cool as a cucumber. And it didn't seem like much traffic was coming into the States—not on the road anyway. It took about twenty minutes to clear our paperwork and cross into Mexico. *No big deal*, I thought as I sighed in relief.

For the next hundred miles to Monterrey, the

roads were smooth, flat, and didn't seem much different from the Texas side. I felt comfortable following J.D. He knew where to go and where not to go.

I was surprised at how big Mexico seemed. Outside of Monterrey, the scenery changed and the mountains appeared larger. My first night in Mexico we spent in a hotel J.D. had frequented for many years. Everyone treated him like family. He knew the language, the towns, the roads, and the best spots to visit.

I knew nothing. There was so much to learn.

J.D. was surprised I took a perfectly good GPS system off the motorcycle before heading out on our adventure. I didn't have a good reason. I just figured there was one road to Tierra del Fuego (the tip of South America) and it headed south. *If I found myself heading north, I'd turn around!*

A computer chip designer by profession, J.D. gave me a puzzled look. We got along, and he took me under his wing. He tried to teach me as much as he could about road conditions, speed, and the proper spacing between traffic.

A year later, he admitted a bit of concern about my adventure to Argentina. I'm glad he didn't tell me sooner.

HORSETAIL FALLS

OUR FIRST STOP in Mexico was Horsetail Falls, located just south of Monterrey. I posted a picture on Facebook, and a lady asked if she could send it to her parents, who were celebrating their 50th wedding anniversary. They were married at Horsetail Falls.

This was my first glimpse at the impact my trip was having. I learned to post on Instagram and Facebook, and a small loyal following was beginning.

The first two weeks of our journey, we would ride, eat, sleep, and repeat. We crisscrossed the country to places like Pyramid of the Sun and Francisco Mazapa. Towns like Linares, Galeana, Aramberri, and Cuidad Del Maiz were all captivating. Watching the birds fly out of The Cave of Swallows by the millions in Aquismon, Mexico, was something I'll never forget. Xilitla and the Sir Edward James' water gardens is a treat worth seeing. And stopping in the town of San Miguel to celebrate the New Year in their town square was a treat in front of the Grand Neogothic 17th Century Church Cathedral.

It was there we met up with Jimmy, another rider from Texas. I tried to keep up with J.D. and Jimmy on an eight-hour ride through the mountains, but altitude hit me like a bug on a windshield. At about 8,000 feet above sea level, I started feeling lightheaded and dizzy. I tried my best to keep up as they zoomed effortlessly around the mountain curves at ninety miles an hour, but I was the weak link.

So many times in life we feel inadequate, like we don't belong, we're not ready, or we've bitten off more than we can chew. My fellow riders were very gracious and waited for me when I lagged behind. At this point, I was so tired and dehydrated they even waited while I rested for thirty minutes to drink water and sleep.

Patience and kindness were a lifesaver for me on this maiden voyage. Come to think of it... they always have been.

Here were two very experienced riders leading a novice through the mountains, presumably on his way to Argentina. Even my motorcycle, the Iron Horse, was patient with me. I dropped my bike a couple of times, which is what happens to rookie riders when they take a heavy bike too slowly around a turn.

TRAINING WHEELS OFF

AS JIMMY WAVED goodbye to us, I could read his mind. *Are you crazy, Dirk?*

The unspoken thought from all three of us was, *Maybe he will grow into the ride.* Even my motorcycle would concur. J.D. decided later, *Maybe he's just crazy enough to make it.*

Every new day brought hope and optimism. I've always been one not to look too far ahead, in riding and in life. I only plan to the end of the road and worry about what's around the bend later.

One road I really enjoyed riding was the road to Xilita—a beautiful mountain village that reminded me of Costa Rica.

Some of the best street tacos can be found in Xilita. It's a destination not many foreigners visit and almost no one from the US visits. Xilita isn't far off Highway 85 or the Pan American Highway. I'd highly recommend a visit to this gem of a mountain village.

We pulled up to the El Castillo Hotel, which had once been the home of Sir Edward James of Scotland.

The hotel was owned by a Mexican family who had befriended Sir Edward. Today, it's operated by Louisa, whose grandparents had owned the house and had traveled the world with Sir Edward. He ended up buying land, and as an architect, he built a magnificent water garden with buildings and structures weaving around in a maze.

My favorite structure was the stairway to nowhere. Literally, a circular stairway to nowhere. A day or two could be spent exploring all the art coming to life in a garden of waterfalls and meandering trails.

One night while visiting the town of Aramberri, about three hundred sixty miles from Xilita, I enjoyed some conversation with a proprietor.

"We are open for visitors, but the Americans no come."

We Americans tend to visit Cancun and a few beach locations in Mexico, but the rest of the country is unattended by tourists from the US. Fear of the cartels and of the unknown around the corner has kept too many of us away.

But the people are wonderful, the roads are excellent, and the scenery is magnificent. I experienced terrain from all over Central and South America—in Mexico!

Yes, Mexico is at war with itself. It must heal itself from within. It must solve its problems with the cartels and drugs. It must solve its immigration problems from the north and south. Mexico is viewed as "big brother" by its neighbors from Central and South America, but it's often viewed as a "little brother" by the USA.

DIRK WEISIGER

What can we do to get over our fear of Mexico? I suggest we give Mexico a chance. Get in your car and drive through the country.

In San Miguel, I met a couple, who were from Oregon. They own a home in San Miguel where they live for six months of the year. Every year, they drive from Oregon to Mexico. Family and friends think they're crazy, but they've never had a problem. This was a recurring theme on my trip.

HELLO AND GOODBYE, OAXACA

AS WE POINTED our bikes toward Oaxaca, I was reminded this is where I'd say goodbye to J.D. My trip was about to become more real.

While heading into Oaxaca, we decided our last meal would be steak and wine to celebrate this part of our journey together. It had been an awesome two weeks, and I felt more confident as a rider. Although I still felt a bit "over my skis," the motorcycle was more than enough to make the trip and make up for my inexperience.

Oaxaca is a beautiful mountain village and an interesting place to visit. I met a blind violin player on the town square. He would play you a tune for a donation. Sadness was in his eyes, but the joy of playing was in his heart.

J.D. had to head back to work and faced a three-day ride to the border. That night, during our celebration dinner, he was gracious with praise of my improvements. Then he paused, and his expression shifted.

"You've really improved as a rider, Dirk. But it's a long, hard trip ahead. There's no shame in going back to Austin with me."

I considered his counsel and said I'd let him know the next morning.

RECOUNTING THE COST

THAT NIGHT, I thought back on my life.

The time I climbed Kilimanjaro. I wasn't really ready.

When I started selling Long-Term Care insurance. I wasn't really ready.

When I got married, and we had two great children. I wasn't ready.

Selling Bibles door to door and attending college. I wasn't ready.

You see the picture. Had I ever been completely ready?

LIFE LESSON: We're never really ready for anything, and we won't know until we try. Try, and you'll figure it out. The confidence you gain will be invaluable as you reach heights you never dreamed.

We don't wait until all the lights are green before we head to town. I had a dream to explore all the way to Tierra del Fuego, not just to the southern tip of Mexico.

The next day, I thanked J.D. for all he'd done, but

the Iron Horse and I would be heading to Guatemala.

Months later, he admitted to watching me ride away and wondered if he'd ever see me again.

That night, I arrived in Tehuantepec and couldn't find a hotel with secure parking. The first night out on my own, and I couldn't find a decent hotel! Beta and Tomas ran a small hotel on the main street. They assured me they would stand watch over my bike all night while I slept. So I checked in. Restless, I checked on them all night.

I couldn't call J.D. and tell him the bike had been stolen on my first night alone! Every time I checked, one of my hosts was setting in a chair watching the Iron Horse, which was chained to a light post on the main street of Tehuantepec.

TRAVEL TIP: Always check the town square and stay in a hotel where travelers with cars would stay. There are always secure, fenced-in parking for autos.

This was a dangerous country all right. Dangerous to my preconceived ideas.

I wanted to pay them extra the next morning, but they wouldn't hear of it. "We gave you our word," they said. Besides, they were very impressed the loco gringo was making his way through Mexico and on to Argentina.

Maybe I was just crazy enough to make it to Guatemala, which was as far as I could see down the road.

The morning air was crisp and beautiful, I was full

of street breakfast tacos, and the Iron Horse purred like a kitten as we headed toward the Guatemalan border.

I didn't have a care in the world. Little did I know, danger lay ahead.

THREE

GUATEMALA THE WILD FRONTIER

THIS WAS MY first border crossing alone, and it required about two hours' worth of patience to have all the paperwork completed. Not quite as smooth as entering Mexico. When heading from Mexico to Guatemala, one must first check out of the current country before entering the new country.

The first person I encountered in Guatemala was a money changer. He had slicked-back hair, wore a blue plaid shirt, and pointed toed cowboy boots. He was also sporting a pearl-handled, silver six-shooter that hung from his holster for all the world to see. This guy had money, relatively speaking, and wasn't afraid to show it off.

Everyone seemed to know him, even the shoeshine boy, who seemed to take a liking to me. This young boy followed me everywhere. For a few minutes, I seemed to be as popular as the money changer during my stop in the border town of La Mesilla, Guatemala.

Okay, it was really my motorcycle drawing the crowd. Even Miss Guatemala singled us out and wanted a picture of the motorcycle...with her in the picture, of course. I actually think she was a tourist from Mexico, but claiming the title of Miss Guatemala will certainly get you a picture with the Iron Horse. Regardless, she welcomed me to the country.

As I headed up the two-lane road with a hundred dollars' worth of Guatemalan money, I wondered what great adventure lurked around the bend, and it wouldn't be long before I found out.

Almost immediately after crossing the border into Guatemala, something seemed different. Guatemala was like entering the old west. The roads were smaller two-lane highways instead of the larger four lanes in Mexico. There were also a few more potholes.

HIGH NOON

I RODE INTO Sanarate around high noon with the music to the movie *High Plains Drifter* whistling in my head. I felt like a motorized version of Clint Eastwood. I'm pretty sure I was squinting too. A few padres wandered the streets while the wind blew a couple of tumbleweeds right on cue across my path.

Pulling up to the El Paso Hotel, I stopped, but there was no sign of life. With the name like El Paso Hotel, and since I'm from Texas, I had to take a picture. The hotel reminded me of a movie set featuring this big hotel in a hot, dusty town that could've been from a hundred years ago. And even though the property looked deserted, I didn't feel alone.

As I swung back onto the motorcycle, a lone

gunman appeared from behind the building carrying a sawed-off shotgun.

In my storm trooper riding suit, I probably looked like a *Star Wars* character. He wasn't pointing the gun at anyone but had it ready. In my most careful Spanish with a southern drawl, I said, "*Buenos Dias Señor.*" One lesson I've learned in life is a smile and a slow drawl puts people at ease and builds trust. It lets them know you're a friend and not foe.

He never said a word, just motioned for me to move on, in a silent language I immediately understood. I gladly obliged him and eased the Iron Horse out of town.

> **CALL-OUT:** Let me add how this kind of scene could've happened in almost any country. In all my travels, in America, Africa, Argentina, and Alaska, I found almost every community to be welcoming. Even Mr. Shotgun wasn't out to get me. In fact, he may have been looking out for me.

SQUARE IN THE SQUARE

I'M NOT SURE what trouble I avoided in Sanarate, but so far, Guatemala didn't have the same vibe as Mexico. The roads weren't bad, usually two lanes, not much traffic, less populated, and very remote. As I rode into Totonicapan, it was about three o'clock in the afternoon. I headed for the Plaza De Armas, the town square.

Every town has a town square in Central America.

It's where families spend the evening listening to live music and eating ice cream. The simple act of visiting with neighbors and friends seems to be popular. There's always a church, restaurant, bar, and hotel on every town square, which makes for a good first stop when touring.

About a block away from the town square, I found the Maya Kaiche Hotel, an old three-story house. It looked haunted, and I don't even believe in ghosts.

A very well dressed man in a suit and tie, Luis, was the proprietor of the hotel. His grandfather had built the hotel, and he was happy to show it off. The hotel had sixteen rooms. Although it was located off the beaten path, it had a beautiful mountain vista. The parking lot was secure, so this looked like my best option.

Many people ask me the security aspects of my trips. Especially, *What did you do with your motorcycle when you slept or went on an excursion? Weren't you afraid your bike would be stolen?*

Security in Central and South America is a double-edged sword. On one hand, some types of crime are more common than in the USA. But on the other hand, communities are tighter, and people make provisions to prevent theft. Every hotel I stayed in had fenced parking with a security guard on duty all night.

With one exception.

After a stroll around the town square and grabbing a bite to eat, I settled in for the night. There seemed to be other guests, but around dusk, they all seemed to leave. The parking was deserted, and the area was eerily quiet.

No one was attending the front desk. Was I alone? Around eleven p.m., I was still awake reviewing my maps when I heard firecrackers shooting off not far behind the building. I checked the window but couldn't see anything. It was pitch black.

This was no celebration. The sound was definitely gunfire.

Maybe there's a gun range nearby? Yeah, right. The shots came in rapid bursts with long pauses in between. Finally, around two a.m., the gunfire stopped. As I crawled out from under the bed, since I'm no hero when it comes to gunfire, I checked out the window again.

A few cars were driving into the parking lot. *That's odd,* I thought.

The next morning, the hotel restaurant was full, as was the parking lot. I checked in with Luis at the front desk.

"What was the gunfire last night?"

Luis gave me a long slow look. "Guerrillas, fed up with the government."

"Oh, really," I said in my most calm and collected voice.

I didn't fool Luis. "Yes, some nights there's more fighting than others."

"Did you stay here last night?" I asked.

"No way, man, I know better."

"Okay. Did *anyone* stay here?"

"No, they leave until the fighting is over. It's going on right behind the hotel, and you know, there could be a stray bullet."

"What about me? I was here all night!"

He looked me over from head to toe, and with a straight face, said, "Guess you made out okay. Thanks for keeping an eye on things." And he went on about his business.

That seems to be the way life goes in Guatemala. Any day could be your last, and every day's a blessing if it's not. So I headed for breakfast, thankful to be alive.

CLIMBING HIGHER

AS I LOADED my motorcycle and headed out of Totonicapan, people were scurrying about, seemingly without a care in the world. Being the only gringo around, putting miles between this town's lively nightlife and me seemed like a prudent move.

Another beautiful day led to a fantastic ride into Lake Atitlan. If you're ever in the area, consider staying at the La Casa Del Mundo in the town of Jaibalito on Lake Atitlan.

There's a history of highway robberies on this leg of my journey. One car will pull in front of a bus and slow it to a stop, then gunmen rob everyone on the bus. I experienced none of this on my trip through Guatemala.

I was anxious to ride to the ancient walled city of Antigua. Popular among tourists, I was hoping to climb the live volcano, Mt. Fuego, which appropriately means *fire*. After settling into a hotel on the square, I signed up for a two-day climb up Mt. Acatenango. I wasn't allowed to climb Fuego since it was active. A view from Mt. Acatenango would have to do. I packed my backpack and looked forward to an early start.

At 13,044 feet, Mt. Acatenango is among the tallest volcanoes in Guatemala. Fifteen of us from all over the world signed up for the climb. Nadia from Ukraine, Hugh from Australia, Cornelius and Ana from Norway, and Luis and Patricia from Mexico. Hikers from Israel and Germany were also represented.

Cornelius, the Norwegian, entertained us around the campfire with his guitar. He was quite a character and dubs himself the gypsy viking on Instagram. We would be camping in tents one night before with an ascent to the top the next morning.

The sunrise on Mt. Fuego is a remarkable sight. The sun coming up over the mountain left me in a trance. I can think of no better way to start the day. There's always hope realized with a good sunrise.

In fact, if you're in a funk, allow me to prescribe a sunrise. So often in our too-busy lives, we sleep through the rising of the sun.

LIFE LESSON: I believe the return of the rising sun is a gift everyone should enjoy. It also gives us hope. Hope of a new beginning. A chance to start anew. Have you ever been at a point in your life where you wanted to start again?

Luis and Patricia, who were from Mexico, helped me to the top since my headlamp stopped working. They dream of someday purchasing a BMW motorcycle and riding to South America. I encouraged them to live their own movie and not to give up on their dream.

When we arrived back in Antigua, we all enjoyed a celebratory dinner together. I know I'll probably never see these folks again, but there's a bond that develops as you meet others who've decided to walk their own journey—fellow travelers through life, walking a trail different from yours. Happy trails, my friends.

THE BIG CITY

I KNEW GUATEMALA City was big, but I was fixin' to get a lesson on just how big.

As you head into rush hour traffic, you have to focus and not be overwhelmed. My first source of confusion came when I discovered the spaghetti bowl of highways—with no signs! You're forced to choose a direction and go for it. I was now re-thinking my decision to ride without a GPS. GPS works best in the big cities.

When I entered Guatemala, there weren't any maps available. Do they still make paper maps? As I found myself riding in circles in Guatemala City, I decided to stop at a gas station. No one knew English, and no one made an effort to communicate in my broken Spanish. (Of course, this could've been due to the fact my Spanish sounded nothing like Spanish.)

After a frustrating hour, I spied a Starbucks. While traveling in remote areas or in different countries, there's comfort when you see a familiar sight. *Was I the only English speaker in the entire country?* After a chai latte and no help from the baristas, I pondered my plight.

I know there's a way out of the city. And I'll eventually find it, but since it was three in the afternoon, I decided to stay at the San Carlos Hotel, which is very upscale. It's a nice 5-star boutique hotel if you're curious.

How did I find the hotel? It was near the Starbucks.

The next morning, wondering how to escape the city limits, I had a bright idea. *Go to the airport!*

While driving into the city, I saw plenty of signs to the airport, and once I arrived there, I'd be sure to meet people who spoke English and people who knew how to get out of the city.

With the confidence of a longtime local, I zoomed to the airport and headed to the Hertz rental car counter.

Edna was very gracious as I explained, "I'm not here for a car rental. I'm just a lost gringo."

She spoke English and had a map. "We get a lot of lost gringos in here," she said with a grin. After plotting my escape route out of town, I was bogged down in a protest, which blocked the streets around the airport. An hour later, I headed out of town.

> **TRAVEL TIP:** Head for a rental car location when you're lost and in need of a map and someone who speaks English.

It was good to be back on the road in the wild frontier. I wondered how to characterize Guatemala. A relatively safe country with just enough danger to be an adventure. As J.D. always said, "If there's no danger, where's the adventure?"

As I rolled toward the Guatemala border and toward El Florido, Honduras, little did I know, the old west was really about to begin.

FOUR

FEAR AND FRIENDS IN HONDURAS

AS I NEARED Honduras, I recalled my blog research and the advice from other riders about the two best routes to enter the country. Turned out, neither route was best.

Route one: Enter through El Salvador where the story was how locals string cable across the road to trip a motorcycle, then allow themselves time to pick through the resulting "yard sale" scattered in the middle of the road.

Route two: Enter directly into Honduras where MS-13 gangs in the back of pickup trucks roam the countryside seeking who they can devour. Rumor has it they play leapfrog in traffic until they stop your vehicle, then rob you, or kill you—or both if business is slow.

The vicious MS-13 gangs are predominantly located in El Salvador but also have groups located in Guatemala and Honduras.

Great options, I thought. *Anyone got a boat?*

I chose to cross directly into Honduras, after considering my third option: Head back to Texas. In reality, the third route wasn't even an option. So I rode on to the border crossing located at El Florido where I would be entering Honduras.

FIFTEEN RESTLESS RIDERS

AT THE SOUTHERN edge of Guatemala, I ran into fifteen Costa Rican riders on Harleys. They were headed for Mexico. We glad-handed and howdy'd as most two-wheeled riders do.

"How's Guatemala?" they asked.

"Great," I said. "Just watch the money changers."

"Bad exchange rates?" they asked.

"No, they're packing heat! How's Honduras?" I asked.

"You're riding here alone?" they asked with looks of surprise, which seemed to turn into concern followed by pity.

They never answered my question. Yes, my odds weren't as good as what the fifteen riders had, but there was nothing I could do about it now. I was like the jackrabbit. I done jumped up—now I'd have to run.

BORDER CROSSINGS

AFTER TWO HOURS at the border, leaving Guatemala and entering Honduras, I was getting into a rhythm of crossing into other countries by motorcycle. A very slow rhythm.

Scurry between buildings making copies of title,

passport, and paperwork from the previous country. None of the copy machines seemed to have ink, but that didn't seem to bother anyone. A stamp was given and a signature signed. I guess it went into *File 13* somewhere.

No one asked to see anything in my panniers on the motorcycle or the bag strapped on the back, which I thought was odd. So pay about thirty dollars and be on your way.

I was also becoming more equipped at exercising patience. I never had much patience, so the exercise was tough, and this would also become a recurring theme of the border crossing experience.

LET'S MEET AT THE TOWN SQUARE

THE ROADS SEEMED the same in Honduras as in Guatemala, as I headed for the Copan Ruins. The village of Copan Ruinas, Honduras was a sleepy town and quite small.

After a simple meal of Baleada, which is meat and cheese in a tortilla, I made plans for the night. Once again, I found safe, secure accommodations on the town square.

DOING THE WASH

I QUICKLY GAVE up on washing my clothes in a sink. J.D. had instructed me to take soap in a water bottle and to carry an assortment of sink stoppers to fit all sizes of drains. I used that system of washing once...

on one pair of underwear.

Then I promptly negotiated a trade with the cleaning lady of a hotel—all my stoppers in exchange for washing my clothes.

The next week, I traded the soap to a cleaning lady to wash another load. By the third week, it was the extra jacket I was lugging around. Then the bike cover, which was taking up too much room.

One month on the road, and I'd traded all my extra stuff. Now I'd have to start paying a couple of bucks for a wash. Usually, two dollars was the going rate. What a great way to keep things simple and help the local economy.

COPAN RUINS

INTERESTINGLY, MANY TOURISTS and church missionary groups visit the Copan Ruins. Honduras has many needs, economically and socially.

With that said, I would highly recommend a visit to the Mayan ruins and the bird sanctuary at Macaw Mountain. They rehab wounded birds and release them back into the wild.

With no room on the tour bus, I hitched a ride in the back of a pickup to a local hot springs. Thirty miles an hour, around a mountain road, standing up in the back of a pickup, took me back to my ranching days as a child. Back when standing up in the back of a truck was fair game...and loads of fun!

So far, I was very pleased with Honduras.

PICKUP GANGS

AS I HEADED into the interior of Honduras, locals told me not to visit San Pedro Sula.

This town was notorious for MS-13 gangs, robbing, killing, and riding around in pickup trucks. I turned on the GoPro to share with folks back home a firsthand video account of any trouble.

"Just keep your head down and let me do the talking," I instructed my GoPro audience. So, right before San Pedro, I turned, headed south, and stopped in Villanueva for a bottle of water.

In case you're wondering if my neck muscles were constantly sore from looking over my shoulder, you're half right. Yes, the rumors of crime made me nervous and alert, but with each passing day, I felt myself become more comfortable with my surroundings: gigantic planet earth.

So far no gangs—only friendly residents of planet earth.

THE FORGOTTEN KEYS

I PULLED UP and parked in front of a lonely roadside store and beer joint.

A single, battle-worn pickup truck was parked outside. *There's the famous pickup*, I thought.

But I was thirsty.

It was the middle of the day, but strangely dark inside the old wooden building. A group of seven men sat around a long table, sipping beer.

They stared but smiled as they turned to eye the

Iron Horse parked outside.

And some of the famous gang, I mused.

I nodded in their general direction, bought a bottle of water, and walked slowly-but-quickly back to the motorcycle. As I was putting on my jacket, the front door burst open and a man ran toward me.

He was one of the sipping seven.

Startled, I took a step back as he shouted, "Señor, señor, Olvidaste las llaves!"

Which translates into, "Sir, you forgot your keys." I'd left my keychain on the counter, along with my pride.

I thanked him. And probably over-thanked him. He asked for a picture with the Iron Horse, which I was happy to snap. As we said goodbye, the man whispered, "Ve rapido,"—go quickly.

Shaken and relieved, I headed on down the road.

ROAD DANGER

I THOUGHT ABOUT the encounter, the words of caution, the gangs, and Honduras. *Was God watching over me or was I just lucky?*

"Ah! Many things this tale might teach, but I am not ordained to preach." (From the poem, "The Calf Path" by Sam Foss) I feel the truth is somewhere in the middle.

So much of our experience depends on our attitude. If you're transmitting a fearful vibe, bad things can happen.

If you're in the wrong place at the wrong time, bad things can happen. I never stayed long in one place unless it was a larger city. It's hard to blend in and easier to be a target in a small town. Passing from town to town, I moved so fast, I didn't give bad people time to formulate a plan. If I was in an area notorious for gangs, then I put *myself* in danger. A safe traveler is usually a smart traveler.

CASA LENCA

EVERYONE I ASKED told me to head for Santa Barbara and the lake at Santa Cruz De Yojoa.

Stuck right in the middle of Honduras, Lake Yojoa was a local favorite. There are no buildings allowed to be built on the shore of the lake. Hotels sat high above the cliffs, and small villages surrounded the water. I rode all around the lake until I found the Casa Lenca Cabanas, owned by Orlene and his family, and his entire family is involved in the operations.

Orlene's family had a dream of owning cabanas, and they work very hard to make it a profitable business. They caught fresh tapia from the lake and served it in the restaurant. I stayed in my own cabana, complete with a hammock. It was a very relaxing two days. Perfect writer's getaway.

Located in a country with such a dangerous reputation sits a lake that provides the people of Honduras a quiet escape. *Was this the beer and the hammock I'd been looking for?* I wondered how anybody would ever find this place or if I'd ever return.

I could've stayed a week.

DIRK WEISIGER

PEDRO'S STORY

THIS PARTICULAR DAY was heavy with clouds, but no rain. It finally dawned on me there had been no rain since I left Texas. Two months and no rain.

As I headed into Danli, I checked into a hotel on the square. After a shower and a change of clothes, I wandered around the plaza—complete with young couples in love, blooming flowers, and beautiful trees. Most squares are manicured very well, so I took a seat to enjoy the scene.

As I sat there "people watching," a young man wandered my way.

"Do you speak English?" he asked.

I looked around, and whispered, "What gave me away?"

We laughed, and he sat down on the park bench. I told him about my journey and asked, "What is *your* story?"

HANGING SHEETROCK

PEDRO TOLD ME he spent twelve years in California with a green card and earned a living by hanging sheetrock. He sent most of his money back home. Then, after twelve years of working in the States, he came home to Honduras and bought a small farm.

He employs his family and sells vegetables in the market. He left his country a "nobody" and returned as a "somebody." He'll always have warm memories of the country that gave him a chance and the wonderful people he met in the United States.

"Thank you," he said.

"I didn't do anything," I replied.

"Oh, yes, your journey through Honduras is a testament that you're willing to ride through what most feel is a dangerous country. Let people know we welcome the USA. Ninety-five percent of people are good. It's the five percent that get all the press."

WHAT'S YOUR CALLING?

Life Lesson: They say your calling is always at war with your ego. Your calling wants to impact others. Your ego wants to preserve itself. [From an article by Shelley Prevost]

PEDRO SHOWED ME he was willing to visit and work in a foreign country and sacrifice his ego in order to have an impact in his home country and in his family for generations.

As I rode toward Nicaragua, I thought, *How could I do anything less?*

FIVE

SOCIALIZING IN NICARAGUA

ALMOST IMMEDIATELY, THE roads got better in Nicaragua. Daniel Ortega is still in charge in Nicaragua and is living large. He is a billionaire. He has lightened up on oppression and practices capitalism in the government, which he happens to own.

Ortega is like a giant landowner—of the whole country. The billboards on every highway say "Christian Socialism." The people of Nicaragua know the wrapping paper might say *socialism*, but the gift inside is *communism*.

Nicaragua has free elections and Ortega, or one of his chosen few, always wins. Nine people ran for president in the most recent election, but no one could name any of the nine new candidates. Ortega was re-elected.

You don't see social unrest in the country. There are no reports of mass shootings or demonstrations. It seems to me that a dictator will keep control unless the oppression becomes too much for citizens to bear. There are rich and poor people, but very few middle-class citizens.

The theme I kept hearing while traveling through Nicaragua was, "Little by little, we're getting better."

MANAGUA

Some of the smaller towns seemed safe in Nicaragua, but the city of Managua had a reputation for being dangerous.

The Iron Horse and I felt no danger as we rode into Managua. I didn't feel any of the unrest I'd felt while traveling through Guatemala and Honduras. Managua is a big city destroyed by an earthquake in the seventies and still hasn't fully recovered.

I thought I was in Venezuela as I rode down Ceasar Chavez Boulevard. Venezuela and Nicaragua are linked together through their leadership. Even though Chavez has been dead for five years, his picture is plastered on signs and billboards throughout Nicaragua.

Expats from the United States who have settled in Nicaragua love the lifestyle. I was also impressed. The country seemed orderly—which might sound boring to some or quite appealing to others. Based on my conversations with the locals, I think the people are simply tired of fighting and dying and are content to live in peace even though there's not much opportunity.

Of course, in any country, there are always exceptions.

I was invited to a celebration in the countryside of Northern Nicaragua. A very rich man was throwing a celebration for his son, who graduated from medical school. In this nation, that's a big deal.

Their home was a hacienda, a farmhouse on a hill. About one hundred family and friends attended... plus one gringo named Dirk.

A large porch wrapped around the whole house. Tables of food and drink overflowed for all the guests to enjoy while a DJ played music. The proud host made his way to each table and finally arrived at mine.

PARTY POLITICS

"WHAT ABOUT YOUR election?" the rich man asked after he greeted me warmly and sat down.

I suppose conversations with Americans are rare, and he was excited to talk about global issues. This was in the spring of 2016, right before the primary was narrowed down to Trump and Clinton.

"Crazy, right?" I said.

"No... *Who* are you voting for?" he demanded.

"Well, I'm leaning toward Trump. I usually veer to the right," I mused.

At the mention of the word *Trump*, every head turned our way and not a word was spoken. The music stopped. You could've heard a tortilla drop. The host got up from his chair, and his face became fiery red.

"No one but a fool would vote for that man!" he yelled. "I have daughters, and we value women."

His wife and son stood in silence. Everyone froze. I was shocked at the turn of events. And to think I had

DIRK WEISIGER

almost decided to answer "Hillary."

As he put his finger inches from my face, he screamed his closing argument. "There is only *one* vote!"

HONORING THE GUEST

HE BACKED AWAY and composed himself. Aware, once again, that I was a guest in his home and this was a fiesta.

As everyone waited for my response, I feebly cleared my throat and said, "Well, in our country, we debate the issues and all come together behind the winner. And besides, Hillary will probably win in a landslide."

As if I had single-handedly saved the party, a big grin crossed his face. He spread his arms wide and announced, "Drinks for everyone!"

I looked around at all the nervous smiles and relieved faces. Sometimes, not knowing the language, smiling says more than any words. The party resumed.

As I departed, he gave me a hug and a cigar and said I was always welcome in his home. And I still believe him. It was as if nothing had happened. There's no doubt in my mind I could ride up to his secluded home, knock on the front door, and be welcomed as a friend. This is the Central America I was coming to know.

Come to think of it... I never did smoke that cigar.

COMMUNISM'S TAKE

AS WE DROVE away, the family who invited me gasped. "Do you know who that was?"

"No, but he's probably important. And he hates Trump," I said.

"That was a man very high up in the Ortega's government of Nicaragua."

After a few moments contemplating the various outcomes I had avoided, I answered, "Thanks for the heads up! I hope we're not being followed."

I eyed my passengers curiously and kept on driving. Fast.

USA

I BELIEVE HONEST disagreement and the trading of ideas usually finds the truth somewhere in the middle

I have very smart friends on both sides of political issues. Debate and disagreement are vital for the survival of our country. When one side is silenced and violence starts, our country is doomed. The party of the losing side always keeps the winning side in balance. I think the founders wanted it that way.

The three branches of government and the constitution have kept us from being ruled by a dictator. There will never be total agreement, so quit trying. Learn from the other side and listen to new viewpoints.

Change is slow in politics. And the unknown can be fearful. Fear can paralyze but usually doesn't materialize. Rarely, in our history, has the same party won more than two terms. I believe this is good. When two people with different viewpoints have civil discourse, they find more in common than that which separates them.

We still have the best country in all the Americas. It's still a shining beacon on a hill that everyone wants to reach—or visit. Every four years, we have an election all over again. Be thankful, because, in some countries, *there is only one vote!*

PATRICIA'S STORY

PATRICIA, A SINGLE mom of two boys, age six and eight, wants a better life for her family. With little help from her relatives, and not having a college education, jobs are hard to come by in Nicaragua. Desperate to do something to help her boys, she decided to sell everything and attempt a trip to the United States.

She sold her car and everything she owned and then paid a "coyote" to bring her to the US. (A coyote is slang for someone who helps illegals cross the border.) After many bus changes, she made her way through Nicaragua, Honduras, Guatemala, Mexico, and was ready to enter Texas through Matamoros, Mexico.

HITTING THE WALL

JUST AS THEY were about to cross, the coyote disappeared with Patricia's roommate and her money, leaving her stranded in Mexico.

Since she was trying to enter the United States

illegally, there was no one to turn to for help. She was abandoned and had no money. Broken hearted and depressed, she headed back to Nicaragua.

The kindness of the people of Mexico helped her to Guatemala. She had no money for bus fares, food, or shelter, but worked when she could and accepted charity when she had to.

Patricia returned to Nicaragua through Guatemala and Honduras. She said she would never be humiliated like that again and decided she would gladly stay living in Nicaragua.

But she still wants a better future for her boys.

MOTIVATED

PATRICIA'S STORY IS typical of what motivates those who are "have-nots" to leave their home and head for a better opportunity in the USA.

They'll risk their lives, and sometimes do, for a chance at a better life.

If they can enter the USA, they have a chance to transform a generation, by learning a new language and making more money. If they return home, their status improves, and they have a better chance of providing an education for their children or starting a business or buying a house.

When I started this trip, my plan was that I had no plan. I would ride when I wanted and light where I wanted. My plan changed when I met Patricia.

At the small hotel where I stayed in Managua, I thought Patricia was the housekeeper. She didn't know English, and I knew very little Spanish.

> **TRAVEL TIP:** Use Google Translate on your phone to understand phrases in other languages.

Her only possessions were two bags of clothes. Patricia and her two boys were living in one room of a friend's house.

Until they were asked to leave.

TOUCHED BY COMPASSION

WHEN I HEARD about her story, the boys' passion for learning and Patricia's passion for protecting and providing for her boys struck me. One of her boys wants to be a doctor, and the other, a soccer player.

I decided to help them set up house—as if there was an option for me.

They found a nice two-bedroom apartment across from a church in a quiet neighborhood. The boys brought a bed and an old TV that barely worked. Her sister and brother-in-law knew English, so I asked a bunch of questions about intentions and background.

Patricia's mother is a teacher in the public schools, which are the equivalent of an inner-city ghetto school in any city in the US. Patricia's mom even gave me lemons and mangos from her tree.

They are very good people, not that I'm the judge of such matters. Maybe you've met people who are so humble yet strong that they humble *you*.

Nicaragua is like the United States in the 60s. Most homes have no air conditioning and use only a fan. They have no hot water, even in the shower. There are cable and internet, for a price. Clothes are washed by hand unless you have a washing machine. Water is rationed in some neighborhoods because so many can't afford a water bill, and between ten a.m. and three a.m, there is often no water.

If you work for a major employer, the company covers forty percent of health insurance, and the government covers the rest.

This means there is no coverage for those without a job or those who are self-employed. Hospitals will treat those who show up and usually don't charge people if they're poor.

If this sounds like a good deal, you haven't been to the emergency room in Managua.

COLLISION WITH A CAUSE

THE ONLY HOPE for the children of Nicaragua is a private school. Colegio Bautista El Calvario is a private school that requires uniforms and has prayer time for the students each morning. They learn English, computer skills, and all the basics in a respectful environment.

I met the schoolmaster, as well as some of the teachers, and observed their school day. The values and vision they embody are impressive—and humbling—given it costs about thirty US dollars per month to give a child a first-class education.

My plan wasn't to find a cause or a family to support—they found me.

You didn't pick up this book to find a cause to

support, but maybe one is finding you. The innocent youth must be given a chance to rise above poverty through education and not have to depend on a government that doesn't believe in "we the people." I want to make more scholarships available to help a needy child receive an education.

If you purchased this book, you've already made a small contribution to the scholarship fund. A portion of each sale helps Colegio Bautista and the children of Nicaragua.

If you are interested in sponsoring a child's education, please visit DirkWeisiger.com/About. Little by little, we can help.

What better way to leave a legacy and affect a generation—to find a cause bigger than you.

LEAVING MANAGUA

I SAID GOODBYE to my newfound friends and headed south. Volcano Masaya is a must-see. It's a live volcano offering you a show of fiery eruptions.

Granada, my next stop, was a nice colonial city and the most popular tourist city. It has beautiful architecture and wonderful people.

There are festivals every week in Nicaragua for just about any purpose. (I suspect there are some festivals just to celebrate festivals!)

I arrived at the crossroads of the road to San Juan Del Sur and the Isle of Ometempe. My climb up Mt. Concepcion brought back memories.

MT. CONCEPCION

FOUR YEARS EARLIER, I was giddy with excitement after having taken an eight-hour bus ride from San Juan, Costa Rica, to the border of Nicaragua, and then a taxi to Rivas, Nicaragua.

Everyone in Costa Roca warned me of the danger and told me to be careful. Armed with a backpack, I made my way by taxi to the ferry and took the one-hour ride across Lake Nicaragua to the Isle of Ometepe. I had my sights set on the big island in the middle of the lake. The island consists of a couple of lazy towns and two volcanoes. Concepcion is an active volcano, and Mt. Maderas is a dormant volcano.

I checked into my eight-dollar per night hostel and promptly signed up for the five-hour round trip to the summit of Concepcion that would take place the next morning. Ibis is the local guide who agreed to take me, along with four chatty Brits, to the top.

SCALING THE UNKNOWN

THE NEXT MORNING, it was raining, and our five-thirty start was pushed back. The Brits had decided to sleep in, probably due to their super-sized libations the night before. We finally made our way to the trailhead by ten a.m.

It was hot, humid, and muddy. I quickly lagged behind.

Hiking in your late fifties can be hit or miss. Some days you have it, and some days you don't. This day, I didn't. By the time we hit tree line, I was fifteen minutes behind the group. The fog was setting in, and the other groups were turning back because of gas release. (I assumed they meant the volcano, but it might have been one of the queasy Brits.)

Ibis said the other guides just wanted to have an easy day and take the tourists' money, but we were headed to the top! I let them press on and said I'd be along shortly.

Staying on the trail would be more difficult than I thought. The trail was a pile of rocks, and my vision was hampered by the soupy fog conditions. I couldn't see my hand in front of me, and I quickly became disoriented. I've hiked enough to know *this ain't good,* so I sat down to wait it out. It wasn't long, and the group was heading back down the mountain, and in a stroke of luck, hiked right up to me.

One of the Brits had twisted an ankle since he had decided wearing house slippers to hike was a good idea. We had to get off the mountain.

GETTING OFF THE MOUNTAIN

WE MADE IT back to tree line around five p.m. The fog and rain, along with a twisted ankle by the Brit, made the going slow. My two candy bars and two bottles of water were long gone, and of course, the Brits had brought nothing but their youthfulness.

Our guide wasn't prepared for a rescue evacuation, but darkness caught us in the middle of the jungle. My one headlight had to light the muddy trail for the six of us. The howling monkeys started their war whoop, which sounds like an angry woman's scream. (Don't ask me how I know the sound.)

The long muddy slides along the trail would have been fun as a carnival ride, but this was real. Fear gripped us as we made the two-hour journey to the trailhead. We finally reached the main road, only to be told by Ibis there was no bus or taxi service. It was Sunday, after all.

SIRENS AHEAD?

WE HAD NO choice but to walk the five miles to town. The limping Brit was carried by two of his buddies, and we all slowed to the pace. This was not fun, and might not end well. Riding the Iron Horse at night was dangerous enough, but a pack of exhausted tourists seemed like sitting ducks to unsavory road warriors. My mind raced as to how to get us out of here.

Approaching eight p.m., we needed a break, but we kept waddling. How quickly events can change in the mountains.

Around the next bend, we heard singing and saw the lights of a country Pentecostal church. They seemed to know we were stranded hikers, as the six of us hobbled into the rear of the church. An elder assured us he would drive us back to town in the back of his truck as soon as the service was over.

Each time the music died down, we thought it was time to go, only to find us in another overtime. The Spirit leads, you know.

DIRK WEISIGER

RESCUED

IBIS THEN INFORMED us he would call a buddy who had a bus. It's now ten p.m., and I'm puzzled but not surprised since Central America runs on a different set of rules. By eleven thirty, a 1940 converted school bus pulled up in front of my hostel. A five-hour round trip to the top of Concepcion turned into a thirteen and a half hour ordeal.

Never take for granted reaching the summit of any mountain. It's a privilege when we make it to the top. I vowed to revisit and give it another go someday.

ANOTHER CROSSROADS

AS I SAT on the Iron Horse eyeing Ometepe, I had to decide. A turn to the right would take me to San Juan Del Sur and the beach. Left would take me to Ometepe and another crack at Concepcion.

The weather was great. I turned and pointed the Iron Horse down the road. I thought about my choice to head to the beach. Concepcion still waits, as mountains do—defiant and unconquered. I decided to keep it that way.

In many ways, Nicaragua remains defiant and unconquered. A communist haven in a world headed in a different direction. The future is unknown for Nicaragua. Come to think of it... we just had an election. Isn't life unknown for all of us?

NICARAGUA

PEÑAS BLANCAS

LIBERA

COSTA RICA

SAN JOSE

SAN ISIDRO

PANAMA

PASO CANOAS

Six

COSTA RICA: HOME SWEET AWAY FROM HOME

AS I ENTERED into Costa Rica, I carried many emotions. Having spent the better part of the last three years in Costa Rica, I felt very much at home.

In 2012, my good friend Paul called and asked if I'd like to meet him for dinner in Costa Rica. The next morning, I was on a plane. The country captivated me so much, I co-rented an apartment with Paul and commuted back and forth to the States for the next three years while working my insurance business online.

I've ridden all over this country by motorcycle, even learning to ride my first motorcycle in Costa Rica in 2012, thanks to Paul. He suggested a motorcycle over a car as a mode of transportation and taught me to ride since I had never ridden a motorcycle before.

Little did I know, five years later, I'd be riding to the bottom of the world.

Our first ride together on a muddy road, straight uphill. I became stuck in a creek and was afraid to move. "Act like it's a horse and cowboy up,"

Paul yelled. "The motorcycle will do all the work."

Good advice. I've been *cowboying* up ever since.

HOSPITALITY

MY TRIP TO Tierra del Fuego wouldn't have happened had I not had the experience of riding motorcycles in Costa Rica. As I rode through the countryside of the Northern Costa Rica, I was surrounded by sprawling ranches.

The Pacific side of Costa Rica has a string of beautiful beaches with mountains dipping their toes into the water. The Eastern side of the country has a Caribbean flare and Rastafarian beaches. Both sides of the country and everything in between carry a chilled, laid-back vibe.

The government of Costa Rica struggles with different issues, like the rest of Central America, but they have a lock on public relations and tourism. The US and China are their two biggest allies, and with no army since 1948, that's a good combination.

Nobody messes with this country. Nobody.

ANDREAS, LEO, AND GERMAN

ANDREAS AND HIS entire family will always have a special place in my heart. They were invaluable when I arrived in Costa Rica. They helped set up places to live, solved computer problems, and arranged tourist excursions.

There weren't any problems Andreas couldn't

solve. He lived in an apartment next door with some buddies. I taught them to play Texas Hold'em and won all their money until they learned the game.

Then we switched poker games, and they finally figured out the routine, so we quit playing.

If you ever visit Costa Rica, consider the town of Jaco as one of your main stops. (Look up German— pronounced "ermine"—at Wahoo Adventures for all your tour needs.) Jaco has it all. Anything you desire to experience can be accomplished from this seaside village. Overall, it's my favorite place to visit in this friendly country.

Jaco has deep sea fishing for tuna (or just fishing), Jeep tours, hiking through the mountain rain forests of Manuel Antonio, soaking in the volcano hot springs of Mt. Arenal, zip line and hanging bridge adventures, and canyoning waterfalls. Even the best value hotels can be reserved by contacting German.

I met German when he found Paul and me a good deal on a hotel and on a rental car. I locked the keys in the car, and German came to the rescue. He called in two Colombian friends who were very skilled at unlocking cars. They had the door open without a scratch in ten seconds. I'm not sure of their day job, but we did appreciate the service.

After flying into San Jose, Costa Rica, I always contact Leo Jimenez Alpizar who lives in Piedades de Santa Ana, Costa Rica. Leo's hacienda, Casa Santorini, is located approximately thirty minutes from the airport.

He can watch your plane land from the mountains above the airport and be there to pick you up by the time you move through customs and baggage claim. Your trip can be pre-planned, and your jet lag can be reduced by visiting Leo. He can be found on Airbnb or Facebook. He rents out cabanas and rooms in private homes.

Leo has to be one of the most honest people I've ever met. He even made accommodation arrangements for me when I arrived in Lima, Peru! Travel is a pleasure when you meet great people.

When trekking through Central and South America, you'll meet plenty of good people. Can you imagine asking the front desk clerk at a US chain hotel about recommendations on where to stay in another city? Or another country? Me neither. But that's exactly why you should visit places like this.

TRAVEL TIP: Keep in touch with the people you meet. You never know when a contact will come in handy.

CHIRRIPO

I SAT IN Cafe de Bocadillos in downtown San Isidro on a Sunday, enjoying my last *cervas* (beer) of the day. I'd been planning to hike up a mountain named *Chirripo*. Chirripo is located in the Chirripo National Park and rising to 12,500 feet, it's the tallest mountain in Costa Rica.

After one year of planning this hike, my nephew Leighton decided to join me on the adventure. Leighton is a veteran hiker and only twenty-five years old, so I was hoping to keep up with him.

Because of scheduling conflicts, we ended up hiking during the "rainy season." Translation: Chance of rain—100%.

We hired a veteran guide, Katia, who would lead us to the top of the mountain. Katia also supplied our tickets and food for the four-day journey. Reservations must be made in advance to hike Chirripo.

Leighton and I caught a bus to San Gerardo and started out on our hike the next day.

THE HIKE

WE STARTED OFF from the trailhead at five thirty in the morning. The trailhead sits at 4,950 feet. The first two hours of our hike were on private property, so we made sure to stay on the path. The weather was good, but it had rained the day before, making the trails muddy.

After our second stop to rest—on my account— we never saw Leighton again. He waits for no man! Who says wisdom and experience make up for youth? If that were true, Michael Jordan would still be playing basketball.

Katia and I hiked about ten more miles, all up a steep grade. We hiked to 10,000 feet for an overnight stay in a base camp, which consisted of some old barracks. Each room was sparse and contained a set of bunk beds.

Leighton had arrived at our 10,000-feet overnight basecamp around twelve thirty p.m. while Katia and I strolled in around two thirty. We were fortunate not to have any rain. It was the perfect day to hike this spectacular mountain.

Every February, there is a race to the upper basecamp, and back down. The record time is three and a half hours—round trip. We were attempting to hike the entire mountain in three and a half *days*. I still have some work to do.

Thankfully, there were no injuries in our party, and Katia was very patient.

THE TORTOISE AND THE HARES

THE SECOND DAY of our hike to the summit started early—with rain and fog. And it was pitch black.

We started out for the top of Chirripo at two forty-five a.m. Leighton was in the lead with Katia and me following. After an hour of hiking, we arrived in Rabbit Valley.

Rabbit Valley used to be a sanctuary for rabbits. They moved the sanctuary many years earlier, but the area was still knee-deep in them, being rabbits and all.

We turned left at Rabbit Valley and headed straight up the remaining 2,500 feet.

THE SUMMIT

HALFWAY UP THE trail to the summit, we could finally turn the headlamps off and see the trail. Hiking with a light on your head is sort of like hiking in a tunnel. Unless the stars and moon are visible, all that's illuminated is the area around your light.

There's a lesson in this story—if we stay focused on the path ahead, we'll reach the destination.

I knew we might not see the sunrise since the rain and the fog was surrounding us.

Leighton made the summit at five fifteen a.m., and Katia and I arrived at five forty.

I decided to practice my ritual of rope spinning, which I do on the top of each mountain of significance. I entertained a couple from California who arrived when we did. They hadn't seen a rope trick on top of a mountain before.

On the summit, the wind blew, and the fog gave off a sort of loneliness, but the destination was no less spectacular.

Mountain climbing is not scripted. *You take what the mountain gives you*, according to my nephew, Leighton.

Tents and fires aren't allowed on Chirripo. About twenty years ago, a dropped cigarette triggered a fire that burned a huge swath of the national park.

Even though they found the fire-starter, Costa Rica did nothing to prosecute the culprit.

THE DESCENT

ON THE THIRD day, we headed down the mountain. Departing at six thirty in the morning, we arrived at the trailhead around noon.

Climbing up the mountain is a challenge for the heart and for your stamina. Heading down the mountain is hard on the feet and joints. Both ways are challenging.

Chirripo was a tough hike. It's an advanced trail and not to be taken lightly. To reach the first base camp at 10,000 feet requires a nine-mile hike. Then there were another three miles to the summit.

I suggest googling the dates the park is open or emailing chirripotours@hotmail.com and chat with Katia. She made the trip worthwhile and spared us many potential headaches. (*Thank you, Katia. And thanks, Leighton, for sharing this experience.*)

I hope you will come to love Costa Rica as much as I do.

Sometimes it's the journey and not the destination we remember.

Hiking gets harder as I get older, but it also gets more rewarding because it reminds me of the struggles I've experienced.

Though you may be aching, hungry, and out of energy, if you persevere in your struggle to the top, the journey is worth it.

BRIAN AND LAURA

TWO OF MY biggest fans are Brian and Laura. They also worry about me the most because they're my children.

I'm so proud of them. Brian is a staff sergeant in the U.S. Air Force. His service to our country makes me overflow with thankfulness.

Laura is beginning her career in the advertising industry and is off to a promising start. Both are very successful and have been so supportive of my adventure travel.

Often while traveling, there comes a time when support is needed.

For me, it's not helicopter evacuation—yet. It's in the areas of social media and computer intelligence. Brian has been supportive and is willing to help me anytime, anywhere. Laura has been invaluable in teaching me how social media is used to advance a cause.

They both agree I'm cursed with the challenge of navigating computers and social media. I'd have to agree.

SHOWING OFF COSTA RICA

MY TWO FANS decided to meet me in Costa Rica and see what all the fuss was about.

We enjoyed a week of stand-up-paddle boarding (SUP) in Samara on the Pacific coast. This was the exact location an earthquake hit several years ago. A tsunami alert went out, but thankfully, the wave never materialized.

We also enjoyed one of my favorite places: Mt. Arenal. The hot springs at the base or the mountain are fed from a live volcano, and the thermal waters are healing and relaxing.

We hiked the hanging bridges and enjoyed zip-lining and canyoning, which also included repelling down a waterfall.

It was an amazing week spent with my two biggest fans.

DIRK WEISIGER

As we headed for the airport, I realized how quickly they've grown up. I remembered our first ski trip together.

They both learned to ski when they were about five years old. I remembered the time Brian and I went on a three-day white water rafting trip in Colorado, and I got altitude sickness.

I've hiked all of Colorado, and he has skied and hiked a lot of it. Brian started tagging along on my adventures when he was seven years old. I was going to show him how to handle the rivers around Buena Vista, but I got so sick I couldn't get out of the tent.

He blamed it on the cigars and whiskey.

I blamed it on stupidity.

But now they're off on their own adventures—to ride their own journeys and live their own movies. They'll make their share of mistakes, but isn't that part of the adventure?

FOR THE BIRDS

AS I CONTINUED on my journey, I found myself outside of San Vito, Costa Rica, near the Panama border. I heard there was a bird sanctuary that rented dorm rooms and had a cafeteria.

I arrived around three in the afternoon, so it was my usual time to get the lay of the land in a new town.

As I rounded the bend, there it was—Las Crucas Biological Station, a sanctuary for birds, plants, and animals.

The land was donated in the seventies by Robert and Catherine Wilson, and this breathtaking facility has every plant, tree, bird, and worm you'd ever want to see. Post-grads from all over the world find themselves studying at Las Crucas.

I strode right up to the front desk and asked, "Do you have a dorm room for humans or just for birds?"

Tati smiled and signed me in. The room included dinner, breakfast, and all the sunflower seeds I could eat.

YELLOW SQUABBLER

I DECIDED ON a three-mile hike around the perimeter of the sanctuary. At the end of the hike, I found myself in the main building just in time for Smokey the Bear to tell us all about the place.

I found a seat in the back row by the door in case the presentation was boring or went into overtime. There were about twelve other people in the audience, with an average age of seventy-five, each with enough camera gear strapped to them to look like an (elderly) army ranger.

I felt young, which was refreshing and out of place, but I'd already committed to staying for the night.

About halfway through the talk, which lost me somewhere around the palm tree exposition, someone in the crowd hollered out, "The yellow squabbler!"

All twelve people, plus the professor, scrambled to the window, like hikers running from an avalanche. I ran like all the rest. I never saw old folks move that fast! But it *was* the yellow squabbler, after all!

During the sprint, scopes and lenses were wrestled out of bags and fixed for the watch. I conveniently slipped my 6S iPhone to the ready.

Then I made the mistake of speaking.

"Where is it?" I asked.

That's when Bud the "birdman" asked where my telescope and camera was?

"I got my iPhone," I said, and proudly added, "If you go like *this* it zooms in."

He laughed and said, "You brought a peashooter to a gunfight?"

There were several *shush*-es as we needed to be very quiet. There were *two* squabblers—and they were mating! Everyone knows yellow squabblers appreciate their privacy.

I got the shot, but later found out it wasn't the squabbler. But it was yellow. Not bad for my first gunfight.

No one talked as we trudged up the hill to dinner. I spent the meal entertaining four grad students, telling them about my travels to the end of the world. They entertained me with the importance of collecting worm droppings for the benefit of mankind.

I had about as much excitement and talk of excrement as I could stand.

As I turned to leave, I ran right into "Bud the bird man."

He sidled up and said, "Not bad for your first shoot, kid! And by the way, it's a Warbler, not a Squabbler."

And life goes on in Costa Rica...

SCENIC HIGHWAY

ONE OF MY favorite rides of the trip was from San Vito to Neily. It's a winding road, complete with tight switchbacks and postcard views. After all my years in Costa Rica, I was anxious to see Panama and the city of Paso Canoas.

Could it steal my heart away from this country? Only time would tell.

SEVEN

PANAMA: WHERE OCEANS MEET

SOUTHERN COSTA RICA is stunning with its tall mountains and jungles stretching into the sea. Costa Rica's southern beauty extends into Panama by way of Mt. Baru, Panama's tallest mountain.

My goal in Panama was to climb Mt. Baru. I was experiencing how slow border crossings could be, so I decided to pay a "hawker" to help me into the country quicker. Joe, an older Costa Rican man, saved me a lot of time and confusion crossing the border into Panama.

A "hawker" is one of many men standing at the border and offering their services for a fee. They help run the paperwork and move you through customs quicker and easier. I would sometimes use one, especially when entering or exiting countries in Central America.

Joe seemed wise and honest. He dressed nicely and was organized. Some hawkers are only there to rip you off. It's not always easy to know their intentions.

> **TRAVEL TIP:** If you're in a hurry, use a hawker. I suggest talking with several. I found the older men to be a better resource and investment. Use your best judgment. Never give a hawker your passport without being with them. Pay them at the end of their service and negotiate a price up front.

Joe, my hawker, advised me to head toward David and not travel through Boquete to reach Mt. Baru because of bad weather. David is on the Caribbean side of the mountains, sits near the Pacific Coast, and is flat. Mt. Baru would have to wait.

LOOKING FOR LOS COLAS?

WITH JOE'S INSTRUCTIONS to look for a sign to *Los Colas*, I headed for David, Panama.

By the way, there are basically no street signs in Panama—something I realized on the road after mile one hundred. My map showed many hotels and resorts on the Pacific side of Panama, but I never actually saw one. The hotels either didn't exist or were in the process of being built.

I made it to David around noon. David is one of the few towns in Panama with an airport. It's a good size town and the first town of any significant size you reach after leaving Costa Rica.

No one I encountered during my ride had heard of Los Colas. My map didn't even show the town of Los Colas, not that I trusted the map anymore. While stopped at a gas station, I asked about a nice place to stay and was directed to a resort located about an hour ride down the coast.

The name of the resort? Los Olas.

After meeting Everardo, the manager, and negotiating down the nightly rate by fifty percent, (yes, you can negotiate if they're not crowded), we determined this was the place I'd originally been sent. What a difference a "C" makes.

I ended up spending the weekend at Los Olas, which was a very secluded—probably due to Joe's frequent mispronunciations at the border. The sunrise and sunsets on the ocean were terrific.

PANAMA CITY

PANAMA CITY IS a beautiful, modern, metropolis. I settled in downtown and made fast friends at a sushi bar.

Stephania and her husband Eduardo are from Italy and live part time in Boquete, Panama. They head to Panama City often and enjoy downtime at the Trump Towers. We ended up playing Texas Hold'em and enjoying the sights. Many expats are retiring in Panama, and I can see why.

Visiting the Panama Canal had been on my bucket list and was a real treat. One surprising note on the Canal—we, the United States, had to finish what the French started. You can Google the rest.

Because of our past involvement with the canal, English is spoken throughout Panama. It's a very safe and modern country, and like Ecuador, they use US currency—which makes purchasing and bargaining much easier.

I started collecting paper money from each country when I entered Mexico. US bills looked older and more worn out in Panama. Maybe we sent them the old stuff?

On Monday, it was time to get serious about shipping the Iron Horse to Colombia. My decision was to either fly the Iron Horse from Panama City to Bogota, or ship it from Colon, Panama, to Cartagena, Colombia. The shipping costs are about half as much as flying, so the bike was shipped.

SHIPPING AROUND THE DARIEN STRAIT

THE NEXT DAY, I headed for Colon to ship off the Iron Horse. I couldn't find the proper road (thanks to nonexistent signage) and stopped at a doughnut shop to ask some cops who were riding two-up on a 125cc. It was a little creepy to see nuts to butts on a motorcycle. But I was desperate to get out of town.

After a dual of my limited Spanish versus their limited English, they volunteered to lead me out of town. Complete with siren and lights.

Got to love Panama's finest, two-up on a 125, leading a 1200 BMW out of town—parting traffic like the Red Sea. It's the only way to travel. Once on the tollway, it only took forty-five minutes.

As I entered Colon, I was told to stay at the Four Points Hotel, or something similar. Colon is a port city and very dangerous. Once I checked into the hotel, where I knew the motorcycle would be safe, I decided to check on shipping at the port.

After reaching several dead ends, Jasper, the hotel porter, decided that for sixty dollars, he would drive me to the port to see what we could find. Three hours later, we had one possibility, a lot of futility, and one bright idea.

A friend of mine from Panama, who lives in the States, has a nephew named Abril, who works at the port. He made some calls and settled on a lady named Tea to help me. Tea helps travelers ship cars or motorcycles to Colombia. I was instructed I would have to ride back to Panama City to have my bike inspected at the police station.

Abril, my friend's nephew, to whom I'm forever grateful for taking the time to help me find transport, had a friend of his lead me to the proper police station. Once at the station, I was told to wait for the inspector and look for a guy named Wilmer in a Chevrolet Silverado pickup, who would also be shipping his truck in the same container as my bike.

WILL THE ECUADORIAN

THUS BEGAN MY friendship with Wilmer (Will) from Ecuador, who had spent twenty-five years living in Connecticut, and was now headed home to Ecuador. His dream was to buy some land, start a farm, and grow vegetables. This was also the beginning of a fourteen-day circus, also known as shipping from Panama to Colombia, complete with dancing bears, jugglers, and the nine-foot-tall bearded lady.

Nothing about the port of Colon is organized. It seems no one knows exactly where to go or what to do. Personally, I'm convinced the chaos keeps people employed. If it were organized and automated, many jobs would be lost.

On day four, I lost my patience—and my cool. Tea hadn't provided good information about getting the Iron Horse on a ship to Colombia. And later, I found out she was located in Argentina and not even in Colon!

Let me make a suggestion—you must have boots on the ground if you're going to direct someone from Argentina. Will and I met "Jackie O." halfway through the circus and suggested she start a business leading people through the process of shipping. Jackie O. was a sales rep for a shipping company, spoke English, and had plenty of contacts. She was at the port every day and could work with the natives.

Somehow, the process progressed. We kept dozens of people employed, and eventually, had the truck and the Iron Horse crated up for the big boat to Colombia.

FREE TO FLY

FELLOW CIRCUS PERFORMER Will and I were to fly over the Darien Strait from Panama City to Cartagena, Colombia, and meet the crate in the port. The Darien Strait is a jungle that divides the two countries. There are small villages and crude dirt roads running through the jungle, but it's not advised to use that route due to dangerous hombres and bad trails.

After the frustration and delays of shipping, I'm tempted to try that route next time. Or I might suggest

Panama build a four-lane toll road sixty-nine kilometers through the Darien Strait, charge each vehicle fifty bucks, and scan their passport. Ecuador scans passports, and it seems to work just fine.

If Panama can build a canal between two oceans, we can probably make this road happen, right? But it won't happen because it makes too much sense, and too many people would lose their jobs. If you can keep chaos, travelers will pay, and everybody wins.

FLYING TO CARTAGENA

I FLEW FROM Panama City to Cartagena, Colombia, by way of Caracas, Venezuela—a twelve-hour flight in total. It was a bit surreal to be in the airport in Caracas and sleep on the floor. Since the borders were closed, I couldn't leave the country and didn't want to venture outside the airport.

The video reel of Hugo Chavez glad-handing at a school and factory played endlessly on video screens. He died in 2013. The people of Venezuela didn't know he was dead until a year later. There's fake news, and then there's no news.

The Venezuelan people I've met while traveling in other countries were very courageous. I only hope and pray the people of Venezuela will overcome the hardships they've endured from their government.

After basically a sleepless night, I boarded the flight to Cartagena, Colombia. Finally, I was in South America. Central America was in the rearview, and new adventures were yet to come.

I was anxious to see the Iron Horse, but it would

actually be another four days before it was uncrated!

They promised Colombia would be more organized than Panama. Colombia and Panama used to be one country and are still very jealous of each other. Colombia gave Panama its independence over the canal fiasco. But in Cartagena, we were greeted by the same crazy circus including dancing bears, complete with jugglers on unicycles, and a two-headed calf. There was a maze of forms to fill out and buildings to navigate to receive approvals. Stamp and sign, stamp and sign.

All good things must come to an end, and it's the same with shipping the motorcycle. Finally, the Iron Horse was unveiled, unscathed, and ran like a top. The ordeal was over.

I decided to stay a month to recoup and enjoy the sights. Life goes on in Colombia.

LEAVING CENTRAL AMERICA

AS I SAID goodbye to Central America, I had mixed emotions. The further south I traveled the better the economy and lifestyle. Costa Rica and Panama are popular retirement destinations for expats from the USA. They are both light years ahead of Nicaragua, Honduras, Guatemala, El Salvador, and Belize.

We, in the United States, have no idea the hardships and challenges these people face. Surviving and raising a family is hard enough, let alone having no real opportunity to get ahead unless you are rich or trade in drugs. The middle class is non-existent.

Despite the hardships (and the hard-to-find

ships) the people in Central America were, and are, generous and friendly.

YOU LEAVE YOUR COUNTRY?

IMAGINE IF THE roles were reversed for a second.

You live in Texas. Your family barely exists on rice and beans. Jobs are very scarce except for the rich who are connected to the government. Paying your water bill is touch and go, and the same goes for food. If you're not involved in the drug trade, you have almost no opportunity. You have a wife and kids who look to you for answers and a full belly.

You hear of work in Mexico.

A friend is working near Monterrey and sends money back home on a regular basis. His family has money, eats well, and they have smiles on their faces.

You talk it over with your wife.

It's dangerous to go and will take what little savings you have, but it's the only chance for a much better future. Hopefully, you'll be gone for just a short while. You will return if and when you can. But food will be regular, and money will come by Western Union every two weeks. That's if the police don't catch you.

You'll be in Mexico illegally.

You don't know the language, and you will stand out. But Monterey is a big city, and you can fit in if you keep your head down. You plan to meet your friend in a little town half way from the border of Monterrey.

The big day comes. The van is waiting.

You hug your wife extra tightly. The kids are

crying. You stay strong so they won't worry. Your oldest son is just ten years old. "Be strong, son, and help your mama."

You climb into the van wondering if you'll ever see your family again. As you round the bend, your family's waves get smaller. You finally break down.

The sunglasses hide the tears. But the other men crammed in the small van are crying too.

Laredo is two hours away. As you drift asleep, you realize it may be the last nap you get for some time. As you drift off to sleep, you're reminded it's hell being poor.

EIGHT

BEAUTY AND WAR IN COLOMBIA

AS I ARRIVED in Cartagena, Colombia, the atmosphere seemed very similar to Colon, Panama, only a bit nicer.

It's not surprising the two countries seemed very similar since they once were in the same country. Panama received its independence from Colombia during construction of the Panama Canal. This independence was stipulated for the United States to be involved in the project.

At this point, my journey was halfway over, and I remembered Dorothy's words from The Wizard of Oz… and I too missed my home. There's no place like Texas.

A slow change happened in my heart and in the landscape as I delved further south.

The road conditions improved in Colombia, and the people seemed more similar to those in the States. I was officially out of a third world country. Parts of each town have modern downtown office districts. Much of Colombia feels very European.

DIRK WEISIGER

A COUNTRY DIVIDED

NEWS REPORTS AND Facebook posts in late 2016 and early 2017 showed a divided USA prior to the presidential election. I hadn't even arrived at my southernmost destination, and I was dreading heading back to a cold civil war in my own country.

Families and friends deeply divided by the presidency of one man—half of them sensing salvation, and the other half preparing for the end of the world. Both sides were educated and smart. Both sides were miles apart on their viewpoints.

In Colombia, internal war has become a way of life. The people are just happy to survive. So, not really knowing what tomorrow holds, the people tend to their business. They have experienced fighting and corrupt governments for over fifty years, and they simply want to raise their families and live in peace.

The people of Colombia are tired of the fighting and are tired of seeing friends and family members go missing... forever. We argue over ideology, they fight guerrillas and a corrupt government. The United States hasn't witnessed bloodshed like what Colombia experiences since the civil war.

The Colombian people witnessed bloodshed yesterday, and today, and they are weary. Is this bloodshed next for our country? Or will we come together and right a ship that's veering off course?

When Americans travel abroad, especially to so-called third world countries, they have an opportunity to either reinforce their ignorant stereotypes or realize how fat, sassy, and spoiled we are as a culture.

Will the United States turn toward socialism or complete capitalism? Maybe the truth is floating around somewhere in the middle. Just saying.

Whichever side wins, we'll be better off than Colombia.

THE PORT CITY

CARTAGENA IS A port city on the Atlantic side of Colombia. There are some great beaches close by, and the beach town of Barranquilla is a must-see. Barranquilla is about an hour drive from Cartagena.

While in the old walled city of Cartagena, be sure to catch Martha and the Manhattans performing at the Havana Club—the best music and dance in town. Martha is the best fiddle player in the area.

The old walled city of Cartagena is about three hundred years old and was designed to keep the pirates out at sea. Now it's a major tourist attraction, complete with bars, restaurants, and beautiful architecture. The weather is similar to the weather in Houston, TX, all year round.

A DAISY ON A 650 BMW

I WAS IN customs waiting for the Iron Horse to be unloaded at the port. Sitting next to me was a nice older lady. I guessed she was in her sixties.

We struck up a conversation, which happens a lot when you happen to be the only people who speak English—and happens a lot when you come within fifty yards of me. I thought she was waiting on a truck to be unloaded, but no, the shipping container held her 650 BMW!

It turned out this grandma was actually seventy-one years young. She was riding her 650 to South America from Portland Oregon—for the second time.

Her first voyage took her all the way to Tierra del Fuego. She started out with two other male riders, but they became a "pain in the ass," so she dumped them somewhere near Toledo. Or are those the words to a country song? I think Nicaragua was where they actually parted ways and where she continued her trip solo to the tip of South America.

I sat in disbelief and astonishment as she told me about her route and about some of her adventures. Here was a grandma, who you'd never picture on a motorcycle, riding the same route as me.

She started riding when she was much younger, age sixty-five, on a scooter, then graduated to a BMW 1200, which felt a bit large, so she settled on her 650. The guys who unloaded the crates confirmed it as Daisy hopped on her bike and rode away. They were amazed!

Her family thinks she's crazy, but she loves it.

This time, for health reasons, she was considering a shorter route but hadn't decided yet. Personally, I bet she rode the whole way and arrived before I did.

Well, Daisy, keep riding and don't listen to any family and friends who have never taken the journey. Adventurers have to stick together. Keep both wheels on the pavement and happy trails. Here's to one tough granny!

A DEAD MAN FLOATS

I DECIDED TO stay near the beach in an apartment for a couple of weeks. Cartagena was a very relaxing city and a good place to write. (My one-bedroom apartment was only five hundred dollars per month.)

In other news, the body of a dead man floated up on the beach, right across the street from the room I was renting, located very near the beach. It was approximately two seconds away as the crow flies. My room was located on the fifth floor, and I was on the balcony watching the waves and writing.

The beach seemed deserted for a Wednesday afternoon. Then someone spotted a body floating. "Hey, there's a body out there!"

Hundreds scrambled to the would-be grave. So I followed like all the rest.

A rescue boat was called. Not needed. A young man swam out with a rope and attached it to the leg with a shoe on it. As the swimmer approached the shore, the crowd grew larger. The police arrived, two-up on a 200cc motorcycle.

As they roped off the body, the crowd swelled to at least three hundred people, standing five deep around the scene. People took pictures. (I did too.) Big, bloated, naked, and white. Gasses had formed in the body.

No one questioned what happened. But I did. "He drowned." The police shrugged.

I checked out the shoe. *Nope, too big.* I'm a size 9D. I went home.

The rumor was "someone" might have seen

"someone" jump off a cliff the night before. Death happens.

And life goes on in Colombia....

READY TO RIDE

A SPECIAL SHOUT-OUT to Eduardo and Esperanza, who stabled the Iron Horse at their home in Cartagena. Salt air and motorcycles don't mix. Eduardo and Martha performed with the Manhattans. Martha had introduced me to Eduardo and Esperanza.

After two weeks in Cartagena, my restlessness had returned.

One problem. Busses are being burned and police officers, killed. The consensus from my new friends was not to continue the trip.

Martha and her son Christian befriended me and were so helpful in having the Iron Horse moved from the port.

Martha and her parents were musicians. Good ones. Martha is probably the best violinist I've heard. One day, she picked up a violin and started to play "Blue Moon over Kentucky."

"How did you just turn that violin into a fiddle?" I asked.

"It's all how you play them *strangs*," she shot back.

Martha's mother was a great violinist and played with the city's symphony.

Martha's oldest son, Diego, is a great songwriter and guitarist. He is Colombia's version of James Taylor, and his daughter is already singing on stage at four years of age.

The Guttirez family's dynasty of music is alive and well for many years to come. What a truly gifted family, who dropped everything and helped my stay in Colombia become a great one. Their extended family, Mary and Jose, put me up in the town of Cali, where they own and operate a flower shop.

I'm truly blessed by the people and families I've met who've done everything they can to help my journey. To me, a gringo, it's a special experience. But I have a hunch it's a way of life for most of these people.

And so is war.

The government of Colombia was in a war with FARC. (Revolutionary Armed Forces of Colombia, or *Fuerzas Armadas Revolucionarias de Colombia*)

FARC is a combination of about four militia groups who'd like to take the country of Colombia in another direction.

I thought about Mexico and the Cartel, and Honduras, and the MS 13 gangs.

After talking to the transit police, I decided to venture to the city of Medellin. My goal was Tierra del Fuego, not Cartagena, Colombia.

TO MEDELLIN

I DECIDED TO take the Iron Horse out of the barn and venture back on the road.

Political unrest hit Colombia. A paramilitary was trying to overthrow the government and violence was erupting all over the city.

I hired a driver to navigate me through a tough section outside of Cartagena. There were a lot of police on the road, and for a portion of the way out, I followed two military guys on the ever-familiar 125cc motorcycle.

The one riding on the back had a machine gun. I had the Iron Horse. We were ready for anything.

My planned route took me through Caucasia, but I was told over lunch by some new friends in the town of Sincelejo to head toward Monteria instead. Monteria had been heavy with guerrillas but was now quiet, and Caucasia was now dangerous.

The hills and I were rolling through ranch country. At each bridge, sandbag bunkers and heavy military gear was placed by the government. Real guns with real bullets. As I cautiously passed by, the soldiers gave me a thumbs-up to let me know they were the good guys.

At least I *think* they were the good guys.

No one I spoke with trusted FARC or the government. I hoped there were good guys, but who really knows? The military was keeping the Pan American highway open for business by protecting the bridges from being blown up by the FARC guerrillas.

I never did receive a good explanation of what FARC was upset about—the drug trade, gold, or the abuse of the farmers in the mountains. The truth was swimming around in there somewhere, but I just wanted to get through Colombia... alive. Not my monkey, not my circus.

For some reason, I wasn't scared. But I didn't

linger. I decided not to stay in small towns so I wouldn't stand out.

EAT, SLEEP, RIDE, AND REPEAT

IT TAKES A full eight hours to ride to Medellin from Monteria. Except for heavy traffic and police, the ride was quiet and problem free. I managed to snap a lot of good pictures of cattle ranches and dairy farms. The road reminded me of Mexico, but there were only two lanes and heavy truck traffic in the mountains. Thankfully, the weather was cooler the closer I rode to Medellin.

I drove around Medellin for several hours with no prospect of a hotel. A friend of mine in Panama had given me the address of the Mojito Hostel, but I had no idea how to actually get there. The GPS on my phone wouldn't work without Wi-Fi, it was almost five p.m., and I'd been on the motorcycle since six thirty that morning.

What is one to do when your twenty-first-century gadgets don't work?

I hailed a cab and paid the driver five dollars to follow him to the address of the hostel. In a few minutes, we arrived, and as luck would have it, they were expecting me.

TRAVEL TIP: A tip I used in every major city was to find a gas station and hire a cab to follow to your destination. Show the driver the address and negotiate a price up front. You may consider negotiating with several different drivers for the best price. Always wait to pay the driver upon arrival at your destination so they won't lose you on the route. If a driver wants payment up front, find another taxi. In most cases, a taxi driver will take you on the best and fastest route—and it's better and easier than trying to use your GPS.

Even though the hostel owner, Monica, didn't know English, we seemed to communicate very easily, even with my broken Spanglish. I've found if you at least try to speak the language, most are very forgiving and helpful.

I could tell the hostel was unorganized and not very successful. Most private rooms in hostels cost around twenty-five dollars per night. The Mojito was just sixteen dollars per night, including a stable for the Iron Horse.

There was no key for my room, but Monica assured me everything would be safe.

When I entered the room, I discovered how they were able to keep the rates so low. The sheets were dirty, but thankfully, there were some clean sheets located in the closet.

I chose to seek other accommodations the next day.

The next day, I found a terrific room in the Paradise Hotel for thirty-one dollars a night, and my bike could be parked for free, with a twenty-four-hour guard watching over it.

I ended up staying at the Paradise Hotel for four

more nights. I just couldn't make myself leave! I loved Medellin. The city has inviting outdoor cafes with plenty of good food and drink. The cool weather was a welcome relief after the tropical heat of Panama City and Cartagena. Morning and evening rain showers with sunny afternoons were common, but the weather remained cool. No jacket needed for me, but the natives thought it was cold.

When exploring a city, I head to where most of the hostels are located. The hostel areas always have inexpensive tour options, by bicycle or on foot— sometimes with a tour guide and sometimes self-guided tours. A guided bicycle tour is an inexpensive way to learn about a city while getting some exercise.

An area I chose to explore while staying in Medellin was Lleras Park. Despite the violence known to smaller towns, this city felt very safe.

One morning, I wandered into a barbershop and made a new friend, Daniel. I say he's my "barber in Colombia" because that sounds pretty cool, right?

My barber, Daniel, spoke English and had played pro soccer in the USA. When his career ended, he moved back to his hometown of Medellin. Daniel struck me as someone who could get you anything you needed. I told him I needed to rent a one-bedroom apartment, so he was looking.

Like I said, I loved Medellin. I think I will stay for a month next time. There's so much to see and so little time to see it all.

Although I wasn't under much calendar pressure, I had to continue on my trip.

SMOKING A FATTY WITH PABLO ESCOBAR

PABLO ESCOBAR IS a touchy subject for many Colombians over thirty years' of age. Many had family and friends killed in the era of his drug cartel.

The 1970s through the 1990s were bloody times for the country of Colombia. Those who lived through it will acknowledge but not dignify Escobar. I was intrigued and decided to join a tour to his previous summer home outside Medellin.

I thought we would see a magnificent home restored, but no, it was still bombed out. The walls had holes where cocaine and money were once stashed. A friend of Escobar bought the home with intentions to renovate, but now charges fifteen dollars per visitor to tour the ruins. Interesting, I guess.

On the bright side, the view of the lake was magnificent, and one of the best pictures I took on the trip. As I, and a couple dozen equally gullible tourists, toured the place, we noticed a group of about twenty people dressed for war and sporting what looked to be AK-47s. As I moved closer, the hair stood up on the back of my neck.

Then I realized it was a group using the ruins for paintball wars.

The best part of the tour wasn't scripted. As we toured the pool area, we were told of a spiral staircase that wound its way up to a sitting area overlooking the lake. This is where Pablo would take his friends to sit under the stars and enjoy some, shall we say, "hippy lettuce." We found ourselves sitting in a circle overlooking the lake when two young guys from

Germany brought out some weed and rolled a fatty. They lit it and began to pass the joint around.

I took a quick hit, like all the rest, and tried not to cough my lungs out. Fitting experience while sitting on the overlook that Pablo built. You see, Pablo didn't use cocaine himself; he left that stuff for the Americans.

He ruined a lot of lives, and Colombia is better off without him, but I'll always remember my visit to his summer home.

BOGATA

I spent a weekend in Bogota, a city of eight million. I decided to go straight to the hostel district of downtown and enjoyed their version of Central Park. A bicycle tour showed me the city, highlighted by the graffiti that's world renown. They've made an art form of graffiti, which many cities now embrace.

Bogota seemed safe and was a fascinating place to visit. But a weekend was fine, and I was ready to move on to Cali.

CONFRONTING A ROAD DEMONSTRATION

IT WAS TIME to ride south. Obviously.

I ran into my first road "stoppage" caused by protesters, located on a bridge on the Pan Am Highway, about an hour south of Cali. The military was there watching the action and inaction. The protesters were extremely angry, but neither the troops nor I understood exactly why.

Seeing the police two-up on a 125 with beanbag guns made me smile. Another day in Colombia.

Chants and banners filled the air like kites at a park on a Sunday afternoon. I snuck in behind the police motorcycles but blended in about as well as a purple tank. I looked like an alien in a space suit, but the motorcycles were the only ones moving forward.

We inched along until a man with a machete stopped all the motorcycles, waving them back. I snuck the Iron Horse into the crowd, which parted like the Red Sea. *This alien wants through!* Confused, and with no machete to stop me, the crowd let me ease through.

I looked back and saw five motorcycles following. *Machete guy* figured out my game plan and stopped everyone, except me. "All must stop, but the gringo may go." So I listened! He had become a one-man police force. The real police seemed content to allow *Machete guy* to control the situation. Once again, a smile and a drawled, "Buenos Dias" did the trick.

When I reached the end of the crowd, I turned back and saluted. *High Ho Silver!* Off I went, and I didn't look back.

Shortly after I left, FARC and the Government of Colombia brokered a peace deal through the government of... Cuba. Yes, really. It's still unconfirmed whether my ride through the road demonstration was a contributing factor. I always stand ready to help.

I guess when you have a government that looks to Cuba to conjure a peaceful resolution agreement with the guerrillas, then what's a little wait on a highway from those upset with who knows what? Colombia has been fighting, not only with words but also with bullets, for fifty years.

This incident made me think about all the trivialities we allow ourselves to become so upset about back home.

> **LIFE TIP:** Maybe we should pick our battles in life—realize there are two sides to an issue, and attempt to find common ground. Once we meet our adversary face to face, we usually find we have more in common than we imagined. We usually experience, during natural disasters, like floods and earthquakes, how people work together to survive. When life is unscripted, the best usually comes out. It's a survival mechanism.

But why wait until we're in survival mode?

NINE

STRADDLING WORLDS IN ECUADOR

AS I CLOSED in on Ecuador, the mountains appeared larger, and the spring rains were beginning. Early May always brings rain. I hadn't experienced much rain since leaving Texas, and I discovered I'd been riding through a massive drought in Central America.

I found myself riding behind a semi trudging up a winding mountain road. I plodded along behind hoping to sneak around, but the two-lane roads are very dangerous on a sunny day, and even more dangerous in the rain.

At a sharp turn, the semi driver came to an abrupt stop. He made my driving decision for me, and while attempting to swerve around the truck, I couldn't help but bump into him.

The semi never felt the impact, but the Iron Horse did.

The trailer's tailgate was headlight-high. Snap! As I made my way around him, I noticed he had no choice but to collide. Another semi-truck was coming from the other direction and was trying to make the same turn. Both semis stopped until one backed off. I threaded the needle and continued on.

Night was approaching, and I didn't have a working headlight, so I decided to push on and reach the next town before dark. Thus is life on the road. Everything can change in a heartbeat. At least the weather is cooler, and rain is a welcome relief.

LONELY WISPY WOMAN

I MET GRETA, a German girl, near the border of Ecuador. We were both waiting to cross through customs, and neither of us was in a hurry. She was traveling with just a backpack, all beat up and worn, and a tin cup hung from it like a medal of honor. Seems as though all backpackers carry one.

Surprisingly, most backpackers who travel alone are single women from Europe. Many take off to explore for years at a time. Greta had been on the trail for eight and a half years. Most take on jobs just long enough to earn a little money and then keep on moving.

Greta looked malnourished and was all tatted up. But she was very friendly. We started talking about food—I probably brought up the subject since she looked so skinny. Greta only ate fruits and vegetables—no grains, eggs, or meat—and nothing with a face! But she hadn't eaten in several weeks. She said the fruits and veggies weren't good lately, so she hadn't eaten any. She did break her own eating rules a couple weeks earlier and had an egg—because it didn't have a face.

Trying to help her, and trying to break the

awkward silence, I suggested she needed to eat some protein. I also happened to be eying a steak on a grill at a nearby roadside stand.

"I'm thinking about getting one of those steaks," I said. "But I could only eat half. Would you like some?"

Greta declined.

I felt bad eating in front of her, but I was hungry. I told her between bites I had no problem with eating fruits and veggies. Mango with some salt, pepper, and lemon, was quite tasty. The grapes I had were very good too.

She said she'd been staying at a commune that didn't have much food. I remember stopping by a commune-like that once—mostly German travelers and rather barren. The folks looked a little... wispy.

They all adhered to the Caribbean Rastafarian look with what I call "rat hair." (You expect something to crawl out.) Most don't have a long list of foods they'll eat. Animals and many insects don't fear being around them. It's kind of a religion thing. They've got to feel the vibe.

I'm all for folks following whatever path with all their heart. But I'd never let a good steak walk away, especially if I was starving. I bid her good day as she shuffled away gnawing on a carrot.

QUITO, ECUADOR

AFTER A NON-EVENTFUL trip through customs, I was in Ecuador. I enjoyed a night in Quito, riding in a double-decker bus. In Quito, I met new friends David and Jasmine, and their two pre-teen children.

We toured Quito together, and later, had dinner on La Ronda Street—famous for good restaurants and bars. I really enjoyed getting to know this young family from Quito.

David owns his own auto repair shop, had spent time studying in London, and he knew English. David grew up in Quito and his wife, Jasmine, is from Guayaquil, located on the coast.

There is class envy between people from the coast and people from the mountains. Both feel they're better than the other. David and Jasmine believe the country of Ecuador is better off under the freely elected president, Rafael Correa, as of this writing. He brought capitalism to the country, and he was recently voted the best president of all time.

This is, hopefully, a real example to other dictators surrounding the country.

Give the people a chance to prosper, and it lifts all boats.

The country has witnessed much growth and is now experiencing a period of calm. After two terms, some feel it's time for a change in leadership. Presidents are limited to two terms in Ecuador—a good sign for democracy. Ecuador doesn't experience the civil unrest of Colombia and Venezuela.

Ecuador is becoming a popular place for expats from the US to retire.

The local people are fantastic, and I really enjoyed my visit to Quito. There is a sense of peace in Ecuador I never truly felt in Colombia.

THE REBEL BAR

AFTER A BEER and two meals, I was ready for the live music. One meal went to me, and one meal went to a homeless guy hanging around out front of the Rebel Bar.

He ate a few bites and then asked for something better. Oh well. I felt better anyway.

The band, Marcela Valencia, was wonderful. So wonderful I sat and listened while they played until three in the morning, and I'm usually in bed by eleven. The entire band made me feel welcome. It was fun interacting with them, even though they didn't know English and I knew limited Spanish. We traded contact information, and they became some of my biggest fans during my trip south.

STRADDLING THE WORLD

THE NEXT DAY, I visited Mindo, the center of the world—located right on the equator.

I met new friends, Juan, Diana, and Alfonso. Al is from Quito, Juan is from Medellin, and Diana is from Guayaquil. They recommended some good places to stay.

TRAVEL TIP: It's funny. When I'm in the States, I don't walk up to random people and start conversations. Okay, I do. But not as often as I do when I'm abroad. When you travel alone, you seem to move out of your comfort zone and meet others along the way. And that's a good thing—and a good practice.

When you travel with someone else, you tend to isolate. They're so many great people out in the world, and they each have a story. I challenge you to step out of your comfort zone while traveling and set a goal to meet one new person each day. You never know, it may be a friend for life.

Juan and Diana met in Europe while studying abroad, and these three new friends were young and dynamic—truly the future of Ecuador.

As you straddle the center of the world at the equator, you can balance an egg on a nail. But it's impossible to walk in a straight line. I thought it was the local drink, chinsha, but the locals say it has to do with gravity.

It was a great day, topped off by eating the local delicacy of Cuy, also known as guinea pig.

Nobody was a big fan of eating guinea pig, except the gringo. I convinced my new, local friends to try it at least. They all agreed it wasn't bad, and we all agreed it wasn't good, either. It's all about getting out of your comfort zone.

I ended the day at a sidewalk art fair and bought a painting of Don Quixote on a motorcycle. After all, Don was a cowboy, a loner, a traveler, and evidently rode an Iron Horse. No wonder I like that guy!

IN SEARCH OF THE SHRUNKEN HEAD

I HEADED INTO the Amazon jungle in North Western Ecuador in search of the Shuar tribe of shrunken head fame.

At the last town, Lago Arigo, along the way to the Amazon jungle, some locals said nighttime was the best time to travel by canoe. The further I got into the wilderness, the more I doubted their advice.

The burrowed-out bow of a boat seemed like it would turn over with each dig of the oar.

As we paddled deeper into the Amazon, I hoped for light from the early morning sun. *Are those mosquitos or a bug yet to be identified?* It was a good thing I bought a mosquito net hat during my stop in the last town.

I could barely make out the bobbing head I spotted near the shore. It could be an alligator at best, or a native with a blowgun, at worst. The story goes that a shot from a blowgun will only paralyze you, not kill you. Then the tribe rips out your heart and liver to eat for breakfast.

But there's nothing to worry about... You won't feel a thing if the poisonous dart does its job.

Once dead, they cut the victim's head off and marinate it in a special root and liquid mixture. It's a secret recipe. After several months, the bones are then carefully removed, and the eyes, mouth, ears, and nose are sewn shut. This is so no ticked-off spirits can leave the body and hunt the natives down with a blowgun. They've thought of everything. The head is then left to dry out in the sun. It shrinks to the size of a major league baseball, where it's then placed on a necklace.

And did I mention it's an honor to be on the losing end of the family softball game at the annual headhunter family reunion? The losing team is "honored" with death.

Keep paddling, Dirk. Keep paddling.

LIFE LESSON: When facing tough times in life, sometimes you just have to chop wood and carry water.

A FALL FROM GRACE

A LOUD CLAP and splash right next to the boat snapped me back into reality. My right hand was resting beside what seemed to be an alligator. The gringo reaction is to lunge away from the threat. A native would never react that way. After all, natives are excellent hunters and gatherers.

My shriek and backward lunge took me over the other side of the canoe with another splash. I found myself in the mighty Cuyabeno River.

In case you're taking notes, here's another interesting and potentially lifesaving tip. The Cuyabeno is home to the "penis snake," which is attracted to, of all things, urine. In other words, don't pee in the pool!

Much to my initial delight, I was only in about three feet of water—and I hadn't peed...much. On the downside, I was sinking in quicksand. Thankfully, the

Siona tribe people are quick to react and pulled me back into the boat—minus my mosquito-net hat. The tour guide, Ronal, had had it with the gringo. In front of everyone, he announced, "If there is one more outburst, the boat will not continue, and you will not be allowed back on the ride!"

To recap, I stayed at the Juma Lodge, in the Amazon rainforest of Ecuador. There really is a penis snake. And head-shrinking was outlawed in the fifties.

AMAZON WILDLIFE

THE JUMA LODGE on the Cuyabeno River is surrounded by swamps with snakes and bugs that crawl around at night. Big bugs! I've seen ladies back in the States carrying around dogs smaller than some of these bugs.

And there are monkeys. I saw a milky monkey, a yellow hand monkey, a howler monkey, a cap pachinko monkey, and a big fatty monkey. Rounding out the no-petting zoo attendees are the alligator, the anaconda, the python, macaws, tarantula, and not to mention, the penis fish.

Headhunters had to be out there somewhere.

THE VILLAGE SHAMAN

THE LOVE BOAT pulled over to visit a local community for a demonstration of how yuca tortillas were made, and to hear a lecture by Tomas, the village shaman for the Siona tribe, who've lived on the banks of the Cuyabeno River for thousands of years.

After being selected from the group, probably by Ronal, to have a shaman examination, Tomas whipped my back with a nettle plant and declared there were five things wrong with my back.

Yeah, no kidding. I'd just been whipped with the botanical equivalent of barbed wire.

I felt him blow on my head and thrash my back with a bull nettle, but I felt no pain. As the legend goes, each time a leaf falls off the whip, you're healed of another problem. Five leaves fell off with my whipping. With more time, the shaman can drink a potion to determine what needs to be done to heal the problem. The potion's a secret but smelled suspiciously like whiskey.

As the shaman whips, the whelps tear into the back and release evil spirits. I must have had a bunch of them since the leaves were dropping off like flies. The more challenging cases require more visits to the shaman and more potion drinking. I think I'll stick with my chiropractor.

There were eleven tourists in our group—from Holland, Israel, Ireland, Germany, England, and me, from Texas. The last day was capped by a night hike to find really big venomous spiders and snakes. Yes, on purpose.

The night hike was accompanied by rain, which was not unusual, hence the name *rain forest.*

The dry season, which is during January and February, brings with it bigger animals. Jaguars, tigers, and the really big Anaconda snakes. The kind of snakes that eat jaguars…and gringos.

The wet season, every other month I suppose, brings more water and makes it easier to get around by boat.

Joking aside, a special thanks to Ronal and Carlita from the travel service for an amazing Amazon trip. Of all my adventures, it ranks among the best.

ARYU AND THE PIG NECKLACE

ARYU, MY JEWISH roommate on the Amazon excursion, also had a chat with the Shaman and received a pig tooth necklace.

I felt slighted. I got whipped; he got a necklace.

He thought it was a crocodile tooth until I informed him otherwise. But Aryu wasn't worried about the non-kosher gift. His father is Jewish clergy, but Aryu wonders if there's a God.

"The world has so many bad things happening. And then there's all this beauty of the Amazon!"

I reminded him that some bad people are doing bad things. That's the five percent. Ninety-five percent are good people who want to live their lives in peace.

Then there's the Jesus thing. Aryu struggles with that. I told him sin entered the human race, and God sent a go-between—Jesus. A free gift.

Accept the gift God offers and offer peace to each soul you meet.

We agreed that faith and free will rule the day.

I was still disappointed about the pig tooth, though. What a waste!

DIRK WEISIGER

8.0 ON THE RICHTER SCALE

AFTER SAYING GOODBYE to Quito and the highlands, I was anxious to reach the coast. The northern coast near Esmeraldas was the site of an 8.0 earthquake just two months earlier.

In the town of Portoviejo, a lone building remained, perched at a precarious angle. Three hundred people lost their lives in the chaos and aftermath. Buildings were destroyed because building codes weren't adhered to.

One local hotel owner wasn't happy with the government, which took credit for the rescues the local people actually performed in the aftermath of the earthquake. I know he wasn't alone in his anger. The government officials watched CNN while the locals searched for loved ones, by texting with their cell phones and digging through the rubble.

MONTANITA — WHAT HAPPENS THERE STAYS THERE

I HEARD ONE must stay a night in Montanita, which is located on the beach. This town is Ecuador's answer to Vegas.

I arrived on a Thursday and ended up staying two nights. The four-block area was a bustle of tourists, locals, and traveling gypsies. The price of a room on the main street of activity was about thirty dollars a night, including breakfast.

I chose to stay at Tiki Limbo. The manager or carnival barker, Ivan, sold me on the idea after offering a safe barn for the Iron Horse, and all the fun one could have in a four-block area.

Ivan also helped arrange my trip to the Galápagos Islands at a discount, so I decided to stay. The beaches of Montanita were the best yet, and the scenery was a sight to behold. I decided to schedule a massage on the beach, from a wisp of a gypsy girl from Eastern Europe. My shoulder, which hadn't been healed by the shaman, after all, began to feel much better.

My shoulders were bothering me from all the tension associated with steering and from the position of sitting on my motorcycle. This continued to be an ongoing problem for the rest of my trip and was only solved by frequently getting off my motorcycle and resting.

Visits to my chiropractor and massage therapist also work wonders. But don't tell the Shaman.

I began the evening by sampling cheap cocktails and then decided to have dinner at La Rosa, which is owned and operated by Roy from Israel and his girlfriend from Austria. Dinner included a buffet around a single table where ten travelers from around the world sat and shared their stories.

There was much interest in my story of motorcycle travel from Texas to Argentina. So, after a great Jewish meal, and enjoyable conversation with my new travel-minded friends, the party slowly came to an end, around ten p.m. Dinner ended just in time for me to meet Silvia, a local gypsy, for a drink back at the Tiki Limbo.

Silvia and I walked around town enjoying the

sights and sounds. The stalls of street vendors selling their wares slowly transformed into stalls selling every imaginable mixed drink. I, being the only gringo on a motorcycle, was somewhat of a celebrity. Free drinks were offered, which ended up not really being free.

No such thing as a free lunch—or a free drink. Rumba dancing was popular, and half a dozen big dance halls were packed. It wasn't long until my dancing skills were found to be a fraud. I was given a pass, though, as all were hoping for a picture with the Iron Horse.

Silvia finally grew tired and told me she needed to head home. She was last seen with who I figured was her boyfriend since I kept seeing them out and about the rest of the night. I discovered locals can only be seen with a gringo for a limited amount of time—reputation and rumors, you know.

As the night wore on, the street vendor stalls changed from bars to restaurants. The music, libations, and food were relentless until four in the morning. People seemed to wander from place to place, and bar to bar, the entire night. Around four a.m., the music stopped, and all the people meandered home.

Overall, everything I observed seemed civil and was never out of control. The police made their presence known, in a reassuring way.

The average age of people was probably in their late twenties, with a few older folks, and one graybeard—from Texas.

How anyone in the neighborhood could sleep

before four in the morning with all the noise was beyond me.

GALÁPAGOS

I'M SURE MOST have heard of the Galápagos Islands, and many would love to visit. I'd heard of the islands but had no idea what to expect.

I took a three-hour flight from Guayaquil to Santa Cruz. Santa Cruz is the biggest island in the Galápagos Islands, and it's also where the airport is located.

I visited the Galápagos Islands with a skeptical eye about Charley Darwin and the whole evolution thing. Turns out, there's not much detail on the island about evolving from an amoeba to a human. Most of the information on the tour was about how the animals and plants had evolved within their own species so they could survive in the climate of the Galápagos Islands.

The islands were mostly arid and hot, with frequent volcanic eruptions. The winds and waves brought in different species from Panama and Asia, which only had two choices: survive or die. So they survived by adapting to their environment. (Now that's a life lesson.)

I really wanted to find a bird that turned into a mammal, but that didn't happen. Sasquatch was nowhere to be found, either. Neither did I see a cross-dressing shark transitioning into a sea lion.

Someone hollered, "Get a rope!" Two tortoises had escaped the barn, and a low-speed chase was on. I had an extra trick-rope in my backpack and wrangled them back into the barn.

TRAVEL TIP: Always bring a rope—even when bird watching.

AFTER SEEING GIANT tortoises, miniature penguins —which are very hard to rope, by the way... just kidding—pink flamingos, iguanas of all sizes, white tipped sharks, sea lions on every street corner, blue boobie flying ducks, crabs that shed, herons that hunt, hawks—who are on top of the food chain—finches that fight, eels that are poisonous, owls that holler, feral goats, dogs, cows—which are hunted—cactus trees, and thorny bushes of all shapes and sizes—I was ready to head back to the mainland.

A padre who accidentally wandered onto to the islands by ship, before it was settled, called it "hell on earth." Good roads and trails have improved transportation on the island—for humans, anyway.

Bottom line—a beautiful place to visit. Once.

In my view, tour prices for the islands are too high. I paid about $1,300 but saw prices reach as high as $2,000 or more. It was a very enjoyable trip—made even better by meeting the Vega family. Special thanks to Filadelfia, Eduardo, Ericka, and Eduarda. They're all in the tour business and have lived on Santa Cruz Island for a generation.

Santa Cruz Island is the starting point for the Galápagos Islands and has an airport. From Santa Cruz Island, one can visit other islands in the Galápagos. It's all part of Ecuador.

The Vega family offers the best prices for trips to

the Galápagos. Stop by, say hello, and tell the Vega family Dirk and the Iron Horse sent ya. They'll also show you where to purchase the best grilled octopus.

I'm glad I went, but it's back to riding the Iron Horse and hitting the trail for Peru.

ECUADOR IN THE MIRRORS

AS I LEAVE Ecuador, I must say, it's one of the most beautiful countries. It may be my favorite so far. If you're beginning to think whatever country I'm about to leave is my favorite, you might be right.

From the Amazon to Quito, through the highlands, and to the beach in Montanita, there's something for everyone. And then top it off with a visit to the Galápagos!

But what makes Ecuador so special is its people—some of the nicest you'll find. Carlito and Ronal—yes, we became friends—he was just looking out for my safety in the Amazon. Marcela and Mileidy in Quito. Juan, Diana, David, and Jasmine. Ivan and Silvia at Tiki Limbo in Montanita. Filadelfia and Eduardo in Galápagos. Everyone was so helpful and friendly.

No wonder folks decide to retire to Ecuador. Whether you visit for a week or a month, you'll want to return!

Ten

PERU, LIMA, AND LLAMAS

LIMA IS A three-day ride from the border of Ecuador. Sand, sand, and more sand. The beaches of Northern Peru are beautiful and known for some of the best surfing in the world.

Besides stand-up paddleboard, I don't surf. I saw a dog on a surfboard, and anytime a dog can out-surf you, it's time to find another sport. Or head for the mountains!

TREKKING THE ANDES

THE PAN AMERICAN Highway runs between the coastline and the Andes Mountains. I ventured into the Andes mountain range, which is among the most beautiful in the world.

I remembered trekking the Alpamayo and Huayhuash trails, which taught me life lessons I will never forget.

These two trails are among the best hiking trails in the world. Each route consists of hiking one hundred miles in ten days, which also includes stops in many villages along the way. A one hundred mile hike through villages and wilderness would give anyone a glimpse into a world easily forgotten. My hiking buddies, Lee, Art, Mark, Holt, and Jan participated in all or part of the two treks. Some of my best memories were forged while hiking with old friends.

Not much has changed in the villages over the past thousand years. Raising sheep and llamas, growing vegetables, and raising families—all without electricity, running water, and indoor plumbing. The outside world yearns to move toward simplicity, while these village people yearn to survive.

Every day consists of eating, sleeping, and staying warm.

The people function without the need for constant chatter from an outside world. The temptation for the youth to migrate toward the modern world of music, internet, and cell phone technology is a constant lure. Will the youth hang on to their heritage or succumb to the modern world that would drive them from the only way of life they've ever known?

One day, we almost lost Lee as he slipped over the edge of a cliff. Thankfully, I heard him holler for the rope. I swung a loop but missed.

I'm gonna miss old Lee, I thought. But our wily guide didn't, and Lee is still with us.

LIFE LESSON: Slow down and rid yourself of TV news and online chatter that can clutter the mind. And take more rope lessons. Hiking provides an opportunity to decompress and concentrate on the areas of life that truly matter—family, friends, and fellowship.

The other lesson is to minimize your life. Get rid of clutter and possessions that don't really matter, which may include certain acquaintances. Go minimal.

Both trails are popular routes for tourists. Ladies from every village are positioned along the trail and campsites to sell their wares of knitted caps, scarves, and gloves—as well as soda and beer.

One lady waited for hours outside our campsite for our empty glass bottles to carry back to her village. She huddled under a blanket with her children as darkness sat in.

We asked what she was doing, and when told, we hurried and drank our beer. She quietly thanked us, gathered her children, and walked back to the village.

Oh, to have the grace this young woman demonstrated.

I'll never forget her respect and patience.

The beautiful pictures from the areas we travel are just scenery on a wall.

What truly makes a difference in the journey are the people you meet.

As I sat by our tent, with the reflection of the mountains in a nearby lake, I asked, *What does my reflection look like?*

DIRK WEISIGER

FAST RIDE TO LIMA

THE RIDE TO Lima went by fast, and before I knew it, I was entering a sprawling city of eight million people. Six million of those people live in dire poverty.

I had a contact named Christian to meet. Leo, my friend in Costa Rica, provided the contact. The address was for a house in San Miguel, which sits inside the city of Lima.

Leo's friend, Christian, owns a house in San Miguel and he rents out rooms. I ended up staying at Christian's house on and off for three weeks.

I decided on an oil change at the local BMW dealer in Lima, where I veered into a good travel tip. I decided to spend a little extra money and have the mechanic check out the Iron Horse as if his own father was traveling to the tip of Argentina. He did and discovered a frayed belt, which would've broken along the way. Always practice preventative maintenance. It will save time and money down the road.

LOBITOS

CHRISTIAN AND I became fast friends, and he asked if I wanted to go with him to Lobitos, located on the Northern coast of Peru, where he owns some cabanas on the beach.

Why not? My plan? I've got no plan.

After a twenty-hour, double-decker bus ride, we entered Talara, Peru. Then a one-hour van trip landed us in the lazy surfer town of Lobitos. This was it! I had discovered the perfect place for a hammock and a beer. If you want to escape from life and live in a hammock, search for Tres Cabanas in Lobitos, Peru. I ended up staying for a week. Even hammock life comes to an end, eventually.

MOHAMMAD — FREE MAN OF BARRANCO, PERU

SAN MIGUEL SITS next to Mira Flores, which sits next to Barranco. All are located in the city of Lima Peru. With nothing to do, I hailed a cab to Mira Flores and ended up, at the cabbies advice, in Barranco, the oldest part of the city.

Barranco is a very old and beautiful city with nice restaurants, bars, and museums.

While wandering around the square, I met Mohammad from Lebanon. He was leaning against a wall and called out to me. Try as I might to blend in, I'm pretty easy to spot outside of Texas. Mohammad knew English, and I discovered he's what some call a "free man" or a hustler.

A "free man" has no one to answer to and makes a living by parking cars and helping tourists. He rents a room for three solas (about one dollar) a night. Mohammad has lived in Lima for thirty years and was well versed on the city of Barranco. He came as a boy from Lebanon, with his parents and two brothers. His dad was the ambassador to Peru from Lebanon. Middle Eastern in name and looks, Mohammad married a Peruvian woman and had children. Tragically, they were all killed by a terrorist car bomb

141

in the early eighties.

His world was shattered, and he joined the government forces to exact revenge on the killers. Mohammad spent time fighting for Lebanon, and even spent time in Minnesota, although I never could understand why or how he was in the USA.

Mohammad was a very nice man and showed me around town. We ate sandwiches from a popular, family-owned restaurant on the town square. After a couple of hours, I paid him five solas and said farewell, as I was tired of him constantly asking my name and where I was staying.

I felt deeply sorry for Mohammad and figured life was shattered for him since the death of his wife and children. How many people have I met like that? We all live in a delicate balance between good and shattered lives. I hope my time with him tipped the scale toward good.

As he said, *Every day I get up and relax by the sea. Some days good, some days bad. But every day new.* He says he's finally at peace—with God and with the people who took his family.

PERU—THE NEW AMERICA?

PERU JUST HAD an election. One side was status quo, the other side vowed to clean up corruption and to have no more free lunch.

One of the things I love about Peru is it's truly the last frontier. You can find a small village on the beach or in the mountains and live in peace. People go about their business like they have for hundreds of years.

Things don't change much. You can live your life with few rules.

Under the socialist system, if you're a resident of a certain county or village, the government will pay you to live there. You could be a guard or open a restaurant, for example. You may not be guarding anything that needs to be guarded, but you have a uniform and a nightstick. Your restaurant may not serve much or make any money, but you do need to at least have a sign above your house. The government will pay about $500 a month, which is enough to live on, and they will remind you every five years that it's election time and, *You want to keep your job... right?*

A government representative in Lima stops by once a year and asks the mayor—wink, wink! "How's everything going? Everybody happy?" The mayor is the richest man in town.

If the answers are acceptable, the money for the next year's budget appears. Voting is strongly encouraged—for carefully selected candidates, of course. In fact, everyone had to vote or risk jail time or be fined.

Anything you need can be purchased for the right price. If you break the law or have a fine and need it taken care of, it can be wiped away for the right price. The land mafias take land and pay the government under the table for ownership rights, which are transferred immediately.

You can squat on land, and if no one objects in four years, you own it. Or you can pay extra money under the table and gain ownership right away. What a country!

Power corrupts, and the politicians have all the power. And most of the money. The very rich find it is easier to get along by going along. The poor find it is easier to get along by going along. The middle-class want an opportunity to own something the old fashion way... by hard work and a level playing field. Needless to say, the middle class doesn't accept the government's money.

High regulations and rules hamper the middle class at every level. Sixty-five percent of the people of Peru are on the government payroll in some form or another—free healthcare, education, and one month's salary twice a year for vacation. Thirty-five percent are entrepreneurs, making a living by swimming upstream.

One young lady entered the political arena for the 2016 election. She was against socialism and trying to change the direction of Peru. She vowed to stop corruption like her father did twenty-five years ago when Peru was fighting terrorism inside their own country. He cleaned it up and put Peru on a path to prosperity. But in his second term, surrounded by some bad people, and with no accountability, he broke the law and went to jail.

Peru went right back to socialism. The pendulum swings, and sometimes swings quickly, but the truth is found somewhere in the middle.

This young lady vowed to make Peru great again and not make the same mistakes as her father. She came across as brash, condescending, and rude. She was not politically correct, and few liked her, but many in the middle class felt she was what Peru needed to turn the country around.

The status quo was the incumbent socialist, an older grandfatherly type, who called for a steady hand and measured response. "Why vote for the unknown?" he asked.

A vote was taken, and on Peru's Independence Day, a new president was sworn in. Status quo won by a nose hair. And life goes on in Peru.

Watch out for that pendulum.

THE LEGEND OF CABO BLANCO

MY NEW FRIEND, Christian, asked if I wanted to drive to the famous, Cabo Blanco.

I said, "Sure, but what makes it so famous?"

He said it was where Ernest Hemingway once lived and wrote *The Old Man and the Sea*.

That hooked me. The town of Cabo Blanco is a beach town and sits right on the Pacific Ocean. It consists of a few small stores, a couple restaurants, and a hotel or two, for traveling gypsies and surfers. About five hundred people live there full-time.

After asking around, we were told Hemingway's house was down a road, around a bend, and on a hill, overlooking the ocean. After about a twenty-minute walk, we saw the only building that could possibly be Hemingway's house.

There was a good view all right, but the place was very dilapidated. It looked like someone had been living there on a pallet. After walking around the place, we could tell it had been a hotel. Then I noticed some lettering above the door, "Cabo Blanco Fishing

Club."

Sixty years ago, this place was all the rage. A-listers and movie stars would travel to Cabo Blanco and fish for Marlin. The big Marlin weighed over 1000 pounds! The fish, not the celebs!

Back then, the big Marlin were called Granders. Famous people like John Wayne, Marilyn Monroe, Joe DiMaggio, and Ernest Hemingway, would come to fish for Marlin. It's said the world record Marlin was caught here—1,600 pounds.

Ernest stayed thirty days at the Cabo Blanco Fishing Club to film part of the movie, *The Old Man and the Sea*. People in town swear he lived and wrote his book in Cabo Blanco.

"How do you know what happened?" Christian asked.

"Google," I said. History says he wrote the book in the Bahamas, but I think I'll picture him writing it here.

WHY NOT?

I GOT TO thinking.

It would be nice to live in Cabo and buy the Cabo Blanco Fishing Club. I could even say I wrote this book there!

But who owns the property, how much would it cost, and what would be the cost to refurbish it?

We started poking around and found it was owned by a fellow in Lima, and a night watchman lived there and watched the place. As little as there was to watch. The "club" consisted of ten rooms in a two-story building, which faced the ocean at an angle. The big main dining hall had a fireplace on one side.

With all the famous people who visited, I imagined the conversations around the fireplace. The swimming pool out front sat empty. The rooms were abandoned and empty. Plaster was falling off the walls. Only the structure itself was standing.

I thought more and more about who owned it and if I could actually buy it.

We finally talked to the night watchman by phone. Not a productive call. It was two in the afternoon, and he was wasted drunk. Happy hour started early for this guy. He cursed, and he threatened, and he let us know how many guns he owned.

We decided it was better to call on another day after his drunk wore off. What takes one day in the USA can take a week or a year in South America.

And that's not always a bad thing.

My quest to start this project would have to wait until we could find the phone number of the owner. The next day, after catching the "caretaker" in yet another drunken stupor, we discovered the owner needed an investor, and the property might be tied up in court over property rights.

I learned a long time ago in business, if all the lights are red, don't do it. It might be time for me to look at Cabo Blanco as a nice, quaint, fishing village and Ernest Hemingway's stay at the Cabo Blanco Fishing Club as a quaint, little story.

CANADA, EH?

AFTER LEAVING LIMA, I headed to Chalhuacua and Cusco.

The country looked like Montana or Wyoming. Anyone who knows me will tell you those are my favorite places in the US. At one point, I stopped to eat an apple—that's code for *watch scenery and do nothing*—a lost art.

While I was enjoying the scenery, Ray pulled up on a new shiny GS1200 BMW.

My Iron Horse suddenly looked old, small, and dirty. We howdy'd and sat for a spell.

Right after Ray pulled up, Andrei stopped on his Honda Roadster 800. After howdies all around, William pulled up on his brand new, 2016 GS1200 BMW. William and Ray are old friends from Canada and were riding from Lima, where their bikes had been delivered from Canada to Cusco. Ray lives in Cusco with his wife, Micaela.

They asked if I'd like to tag along. "Sure!" I said. They seemed like good guys and turned out to be pretty good riders. While riding in elevation, where the air is thin, Andrei and William were feeling light-headed, so we decided to stop and rest. Then Andrei rolled on, but William decided to pull out his sleeping bag and lay down for a while.

Altitude sickness can cause irrational thinking.

I rode on ahead to catch Ray, who had turned around to make sure William was okay. The weather turned colder, and I finally got to use my winter riding gloves. With heated handgrips, I was now warm and toasty. Andrei felt chilled, so we stopped for coca tea in a small town. Coca leaves are legal for tea and a local mainstay for the start of each day. Cocaine can be made out of Coca leaves, but the coca tea was as close as I got to the drug. Thankfully.

Llama ranching is the main source of income in these parts. Much of Peru is open range with herds of llama and the women folk doing all the roundup duty. Come to think of it, all I saw was the women doing all the work.

After two long, hard days we rode into Cusco and to the house of Ray and Micaela. They have a nice place near the old square with a courtyard and a safe place for the Iron Horse. This town reminded me of so many other old South America towns with walled villages.

MY TURN AT MAPI

IN CUSCO, I met Ian from England, who was riding the same route as I was. He flew his bike across the pond to Bogota, Colombia, had ridden this far, and was now headed to the tip of Argentina. Ian is a great guy with many stories. He recently retired from the Royal Army and sold his life—everything he owned except his Yamaha 650.

We headed toward our day's destination: Machu Picchu.

I finally climbed my way to the top of Machu Picchu. I really didn't have a plan developed on how to climb *MaPi*, which is what the hipster crowd calls this landmark. My only plan was to drive the Iron Horse as far as I could and figure the rest out along the way.

You can't drive to MaPi City. You can go as far as Ollatambotao and then walk or take a train to the foot of MaPi.

My new friend, Ian, was also climbing MaPi and had accomplished some pre-planning. I said I'd join him. After all, I couldn't have people ask, "Did you see Machu Picchu?" and then say, "Well, no—I was close but couldn't be bothered."

Tour packages to the top of MaPi can cost as much as you want to spend, from a first-class rate to the backpacker rate of ninety dollars. I chose the latter.

When you're riding to the tip of South America, you can't live like a tourist. You have to pick and choose. This is one experience where you might want to spend a little extra.

Overall, the budget tour is very disorganized. We bought a package in Cusco from Mary. Mary worked at one of the millions of tourist shops that line the main plaza in the old part of the city. Mary told us to be waiting in front of her shop by seven thirty the following morning.

Once we arrived out front, we'd be picked up by a small bus and driven to the hydro plant where we'd then hike for three hours to the city of MaPi. Once in the city of MaPi, we'd stay in a hostel for the night. The next morning, we'd hike up MaPi, which would take about an hour. Lunch, dinner, and a breakfast snack would be included.

How hard could it be, right?

When someone in the Americas south of Texas

says a certain time, we know it doesn't really mean that time, but somewhere in the vicinity—usually at least thirty minutes later. I'm sure people intended to show up sometime that day.

Ian and I arrived by seven fifteen and waited. And waited. The shop opened at eight a.m. The little girl attending the shop called a phone number, and after several tries, she announced the bus was on its way. No worries.

Thirty minutes later, a fellow showed up and said, "Follow me." Translation: We are walking.

We walked about four blocks, uphill, to some small buses waiting on a side street. Other tourists were milling around the area. After thirty minutes, an old rattletrap van pulled up. It was a Mercedes but had clearly seen better days.

We all piled in—ten of us and the driver. All were locals except Ian and me. My plan not to travel like a tourist was officially dialed in.

Being a seasoned traveler, I knew there was trouble when, not five minutes after takeoff, the driver pulled into a gas station—to air up a tire and gas up the van.

I took a deep breath, knowing I needed to relax and not sweat the small stuff. We headed higher into the mountains. No guardrails, in an old vehicle, with the front right tire low on air. Brilliant move, that ninety-dollar package.

We headed further up the mountain with the tires screeching on every turn.

WHEN YOU GOTTA GO, IT'S TIME TO BLOW

WINDING ROADS AT high speeds, mixed with dust, can wreak havoc on one's stomach. This mixture decided to take its toll on the little girl sitting directly behind me.

Not even an hour into the carnival ride, which required me hanging on with both hands to the safety handle, she started sharing her breakfast. Mom and dad scrambled for a bag but weren't very successful.

I leaned forward, hanging on with both hands, hoping it had been a small breakfast. No such luck. After a time of discharging, there was a reprieve, and then the chunks started flying again. I just stared straight ahead, opening a window to relieve everyone else of the stench.

Why do parents feel obliged to put kids through this? I wondered.

Then I remembered my own follies with my children back in the day and the tummy-twisting adventures I took them on.

Nothing ever changes the gastro-dynamics of a kid's stomach. What goes in, if jostled around, is gonna come out!

Now two hours into the trip, we stopped for a bathroom and snack break. I looked over and, much to my dismay, the girl was eating again. *No!* I cried. *This can't be allowed to happen.* Okay, I thought about yelling, but I didn't.

We climbed back into the van and moved on. The young girl was again seated right behind me—but with a bag at the ready. Our driver didn't seem to know what the brake pedal was for, as time was of the essence, so each corner came faster and faster.

I don't mind riding around mountain curves on the Iron Horse, but in a van, with a bad wheel, was another story.

At corner number forty-eight or so, the unlucky girl started barfing again. Long and loud. I stared straight ahead, in my most polite gringo posture, wondering, *Lays potato chips?* I swear I felt a slight spray and a hint of barf. I hoped it was my imagination and hung on for dear life, hoping this ain't how it all ends—and that the tire holds up.

Four hours after departure, we arrived at an old building where a bunch of other people was sitting and standing around. We piled out of the van and proceeded to be seated at long tables. Guess who took the seat across from me?

My indigestive little friend, who was about eleven years old, slumped into the old wooden chair. Her eyes were swollen from heaving, and to my amazement, she proceeded to dig into more food. *No, say it ain't so!*

After lunch and a bathroom break, we piled back into the van. *Wait, I thought we'd arrived?* This time, we drove for just two minutes to the train station or trailhead. I felt sorry for the little girl, who endured six hours of a dreadful van ride through the mountains, and hoped MaPi would be worth it for her. (And for me.)

DIRK WEISIGER

HIKING TO MAPI CITY

LOOKING AROUND AT the crowd, we figured most were waiting for the train. All the young backpackers, along with Ian and me, started out on the hike.

After thirty minutes of uphill hiking, we reached a set of train tracks. For the next three hours, we followed a chunky, gravel, hike path along the tracks. It's a rough trail but has gorgeous scenery. Truly the best part of Machu Picchu are the views of the surrounding mountains.

As the train passed, full of happy, well-fed passengers, and one nauseous little girl, we trudged on with our snacks and Gatorade in hand. At about dark-thirty, we were finally able to glimpse a quaint mountain village. We'd made it! It was six thirty p.m. Eleven hours earlier, we had started our journey.

A fellow traveler suggested we head for the town square. We made it to bed around eleven thirty with instructions to start hiking at four thirty the next morning. You can take a bus to the top if you pay extra. I'm climbing.

The next morning, we hiked to the trailhead, slowly, in backpack-to-backpack traffic. One and a half hours of steps, straight up. But we made it to the top just as the sun was cresting on the surrounding peaks.

A beauty to behold. Worth it? Absolutely.

After two hours of being traded around to different guides, we took some pictures and decided it was time to head down—by bus. We splurged for train tickets at MaPi city. Pay extra, my friend. The ride back to Cusco was heaven, comparatively.

Machu Picchu is a beautiful sight. Built six hundred years ago by the Inca as a utopian village, it lasted only one hundred years. Legend has it, the women decided to live down by the river and farm instead of hauling water up a mountain three times a day. As you'd imagine, the menfolk didn't last long on the peak and followed shortly thereafter. No one lives on MaPi now, but the llamas, which are thriving.

I'd recommend a visit to MaPi. I despise tourist traps, but trust me—this one was worth it. And ignore my earlier advice. For this experience, make an exception and travel like a tourist. If you have to hike, hike down.

GOODBYE, PERU

IAN AND I headed south for Lake Titicaca, toward the border to the land of mystery.

Half of Lake Titicaca is in Peru, and the other half of the lake is in Bolivia. Peru says they have the "Titi" and Bolivia gets the "caca."

The indigenous people of the floating islands are a must-see. I'm looking forward to the land "frozen in time" that awaits. Peru has so much to offer. There's no way to experience it all... except to come back for another visit.

BRAZIL
BOLIVA
LA PAZ
ORURO
POTOSI
VILLAZÓN
PARAGUAY
CHILE
ARGENTINA

Eleven

BOLIVIA: A LAND STUCK IN TIME

I'D HEARD HORROR stories of US citizens having a hard time traveling through Bolivia.

Ian and I decided to ride through Bolivia together. He was riding a Yamaha 650, but he knew more about my BMW than I did since he'd owned one before.

As we reached the border of Peru and queued up in the line, a man stepped out from the crowd and asked us to pay five dollars to cross the bridge to the immigration station. We paid, but it seemed odd.

Odd was about to get even odder.

PULLED OUT OF LINE

AS WE WAITED in line to have our passports stamped, Ian received his as they waved him through. I, on the other hand, was ushered to another room because I didn't have a visa.

They wanted to deport me back to Peru to get a visa. An Argentine rider persuaded the policeman to let me apply for the visa there at the border. Twenty dollars to help "the children" persuaded the official to let me stay.

After seven—yes, seven—hours obtaining bank documents and proving I'd be staying in La Paz, and then verifying I was gainfully employed, the officials gave me a visa. "Gave" might not be the right word since it cost three hundred dollars.

On the positive side, I'm now the proud owner of a ten-year visa to the country of Bolivia.

Fair enough, it's their country. It seems the officials of Bolivia simply make Americans do what we make foreign visitors to our country do. As I headed for the Iron Horse, I noticed my backpack had been stolen. My laptop was inside... with all my travel writings.

I was totally deflated. This was the low point of my trip, and I was ready to head back to Texas.

"Cheer up, mate," Ian chirped, snapping me out of my gloom. We had a three-hour ride before nightfall. Never underestimate the power of a good riding buddy. So, onward to La Paz.

GETTING GAS

ALL THROUGH BOLIVIA, I followed Ian through the gas stations. If you're a foreigner, you pay double for fuel, as it's subsidized for citizens by the government. If your home country wasn't on the computer list, you couldn't buy gasoline.

England was on the list. I never saw the USA. They never scrolled down that far.

As we were about to leave the country, the gas station attendant asked for my passport. I quickly showed her my Texas driver's license—well, we were a Republic once. She didn't see Texas on her list.

"Where is that?" she asked.

I pointed to the first country I saw, Colombia. "Texas is a little province in the north, near the Amazon. Delighted, she wrote down *Texas, Colombia*.

I don't know if US citizens can buy gas in Bolivia, but a Texan can!

THE REST OF THE STORY

AS WE PASSED through the countryside, the beauty overwhelmed me.

The landscape absolutely engulfed me, and I felt so happy to be alive. What a great adventure. The air was crisp and cool, the views of the mountains were magnificent, and llamas and alpacas roamed the landscape, free of fences. The only sign of civilization was the asphalt road.

I sensed a freedom not experienced in our rat race. A big, wide world exists that I never knew. I felt alive and thankful for the great privilege of touring this great country. It truly was a land frozen in time and could have easily been transported to one hundred years ago. Maybe that's why my visa was so expensive.

As we rode into La Paz, a celebration was occurring—a festival parade of characters in elaborate dress and dance. It was explained that once a year, the locals take a day to honor their culture, and everyone participates. The dances go on for twenty-four hours.

DIRK WEISIGER

As a guest to the festival, you're treated like royalty. They dance for you as if you're the only one watching. You can participate or just watch. I truly felt like an honored guest. Everyone I met was happy with their country and proud to share their traditions, which had been handed down from generation to generation.

On one hand, this is a country of people who made us feel welcomed and were glad we were visiting. On the other hand, the government isn't as impressed with the United States as we are. We have to jump through many hoops to obtain a visa. US citizens can't purchase gas, and speeding tickets are handed out based on where you are born.

LET ME SUGGEST A LIFE LESSON: Don't let one story be the story. I could share with you one bad experience, and you'd never visit Bolivia. Or I could share with you one of my most positive experiences in Bolivia, and you'd consider leaving tomorrow.

PAUSE IN LA PAZ

LA PAZ IS A city of about 800,000 people. Many of the residents dress as they have for generations. Others seem to dress as modern as people in any city in the USA.

The city is surrounded by mountains and sits at the bottom of a giant bowl. The mass transit system includes gondolas—all electric and all very modern—

installed by the Swiss. The gondolas crisscross the city at the top of the bowl, making it easy, and scenic, to be transported from one side of the city to the other.

A new friend, Grace, spoke English and was a tour guide. She explained how locals were so appreciative of tourists from other countries. Once welcomed, it seemed to me, travelers could stop by any home they came across and be treated like a king. Whatever was needed would be provided—you were treated as a valued guest. *What a country!*

I thought about how we, as North Americans, always seem to travel to the same old touristy places—yet this is a magnificent country, frozen in time, fresh, alive, and strange-yet-familiar. I saw no other US citizens in Bolivia. What a shame.

I would highly recommend this country for your next trip abroad. It is a jewel, a diamond if you will. And was an experience I'll never forget.

I'll be back as often as I can, or at least until my visa expires.

So many times we judge a country by one story, be it good or bad. Don't let one story be the only story. The truth is always in the middle.

TWO DOCTORS: A FAMILY AFFAIR

CARMEN WAS BORN and raised in Bolivia and grew up close to her cousin, Javier. Both their families were of modest means. Living in Bolivia is similar to living in the USA in the sixties.

Carmen always knew her cousin was… different. As a child, Javier would collect bugs and be fascinated with their anatomy. He would hide bugs in the bedsheets to scare his cousins. He was always advanced in school and had a dream to be a doctor. After going to medical school in Bolivia, Javier found opportunities were greater in Chile. Today, Javier is one of the top orthopedic surgeons in Chile. Someday, Javier would like to return to his home country and continue his practice.

Carmen's daughter, Laura, is now in medical school in Argentina and wants to return to Bolivia someday to help her home country. She's a very dedicated student, and I know she will fulfill her dreams.

LIFE TIP: With drive and determination, it doesn't matter where you're born, there is always a way out and up.

SALT FLATS AND DAKAR

I'D HEARD OF the Dakar Rally Races in Africa, but I didn't know they were now being held in South America. The Dakar Rally takes place during the first two weeks of January each year. The race was moved from Africa and now takes place in parts of Chile, Argentina, and in the salt flats of Bolivia. Since we were visiting in October, we decided against a guided tour. I chose to tour the race area on my Iron Horse.

To not only see the salt flats but also to cruise over them on the Iron Horse, was amazing. I backed off at 110 mph so I wouldn't show anyone up. I had surprisingly good traction. Ian claimed he reached 120mph on his Yamaha 650, which I'd never admit to my fellow BMW riders.

While driving along the flats, I noticed a hole dug down into the "lake." Solid salt for at least five feet down, and they say it gets as deep as nine feet. There was even a hotel made entirely of salt. As far as you could see, in every direction, was a sea of salt.

The racers, in the Dakar Rally, race at over 200 miles per hour. Well, I was happy with my 110 mph time trial. I would highly recommend this experience if you're in the area.

SPEEDING... SERIOUSLY

RIGHT BEFORE WE arrived at the border, we were stopped by the highway police for speeding. I was following Ian, but after looking over our passports, the police only wanted me to pay the fine. (*C'mon, Bolivia. I was just saying such nice things about you!*)

"How can that be?" I asked. "I was right behind my friend!"

Turns out, Ian showed the police his badge and license from twenty years earlier, when he was a mall cop in London. Ian's new law enforcement friends were impressed and welcomed him into the brotherhood. Hugs and high-fives all around.

Meanwhile, one policeman was holding the radar gun on me as if it had bullets. They must have just gotten the radar gun and thought it was a Taser.

After the hugging stopped, they asked me for two hundred dollars and kindly offered to escort me to the nearest ATM. Ian convinced the police to take twenty dollars "for the children" and then offered to take custody of the speeding American.

> **TRAVEL TIP:** Another travel tip that saved me money when being stopped by the police was to have a "fake" wallet and a "real" wallet. In the fake wallet, I carried a copy of my passport and about twenty to thirty dollars in local currency. I would use the fake wallet when stopped by the police. My real wallet was locked in the boxes on my motorcycle.

The police always wanted around two hundred dollars from the local ATM, but I'd let them know I didn't understand what they were asking and the twenty to thirty dollars was all I had. Four times, in four different countries, during my trip, I was stopped for different infractions. Each of the four times the police wanted two hundred dollars, and each of the four times I handed over around twenty dollars in local currency.

One may say I was duped by a dirty cop, but I decided to thank the officer for reminding me of the infraction. I was helping a poor policeman's family. If I can spend three times as much for coffee at Starbucks, then I can help a poor family. It's all about perspective.

"Make sure he doesn't cause any more trouble, okay?" the cops said to Ian as he took protective custody of me.

I just rolled my eyes and told the officer to holster that pistol of his, as I swung back on the Iron Horse and carefully followed Ian.

From the border crossing to La Paz, the salt flats, and the wonderful countryside, Bolivia is a land in contrast—frozen in time, yet struggling to catch up to the rest of the world. Some of its people are trying to pull it toward the future.

Most are pleased with their leader, Evan Morales, who's trying to bring educated people to the forefront to help run the country. With people I met like Grace, Carmen, Javier, and the young people like Laura, Bolivia is in good hands. I shall be back, now that I have a visa.

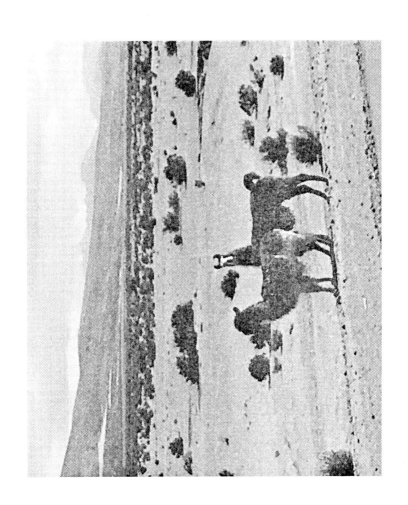

TWELVE

IN A RUT IN CHILE

AFTER ENTERING CHILE, Ian went on his way. Many times, lone travelers ride together for a season, but you both know when it's time to go on alone. That time had come.

I was headed for Santiago, and Ian was headed down Carretera Austral, a long gravel highway deep into Chile.

I ended up following the route later. I had hoped our trails would cross again. Ian was made for travel, a lone warrior. He had once been in the Royal Army in Great Britain. Without children and having never married, he too shared my quest for "the place he hadn't been is the place he wants to go."

He told me of his ride through Thailand, Cambodia, and Vietnam. "Let's ride, mate," he said. Godspeed, Ian, and someday, we shall.

SANTIAGO

A CITY OF seven million, Santiago was bustling. I stayed in a nice part of Santiago in the Providencia district at a small "mom and pop" hotel.

I enjoyed the parks, food, and festivities. Yes, it seems there are always festivals, celebrations, and parades, in addition to the lively nightlife. I actually ended up spending New Year's Eve in Valparaiso with friends I met in Bolivia.

Santiago was one of the most modern cities I visited. Chile has had its share of dictators. Pinochet killed all the opposition but did create some laws, which helped the economy work more efficiently than the economies of some of their South American neighbors.

The subway was easy to ride and made moving around the city a breeze. Be sure to take the bicycle tour in the Patronato district near downtown, and visit the fish market. Of course, one day visiting the wine vineyards will make one appreciate Chile's vino. I enjoyed my time in Santiago and count it as one of my favorite cities in South America.

BMW CHECKUP

I MADE SURE to visit the local BMW service department whenever I could for a checkup of the Iron Horse. I asked the mechanic to take care of any potential problems. I was pretty sure an extra hundred-dollar bill would also guarantee a double check.

I was now headed into the Patagonia of Chile. Not the time or place for breakdowns or repairs. Patricio made sure all was well with the Iron Horse. Preventative maintenance at BMW dealers in

Colombia, Peru, and Chile saved me from any potential headaches and is highly recommended.

CATCHING THE BIG ONE

WHAT'S KNOWN AS The Lakes District begins around Pucon, Chile. A series of tourist towns and lakes dot this landscape.

The roads were in good shape, but I made slow progress—there were simply too many interesting places to visit! Various outdoor activities captivated my interest—from trout fishing near Puerto Aisen and Lago De Los Palos to Standup Paddleboarding to horseback riding, and then hike a volcano near Pucon.

I also went on a rafting trip near Puerto Bertrand and Rio Baker, and then climbed a glacier near Puerto Rio Tranquil. Sounds like a two-week vacation, but I stayed at each place for two days. So much to do and so little time.

Here's a travel tip example, which I dare you to try...

I'm not a fisherman but wanted to try my hand at trout fishing. I was in the heart of the best trout fishing in the world. Coincidentally, this activity comes with the highest price tag to hire a professional guide.

While having a dinner of grilled trout in the city of Aisen, I happened to ask the owner of the restaurant if he knew anyone who could take me trout fishing for a couple of hours the next day—someone who wanted to make a few bucks.

He made some phone calls and told me to come

back to his restaurant in a couple of hours.

I arrived back at the restaurant, and Juan showed up. "Be ready to go at eight a.m.," he said with a smile. Juan would provide the boat and all the tackle.

The next day, Juan drove me an hour out of town to Lake De Los Palos where Carlos was waiting with his boat. Carlos knew the lake like the back of his hand. On my first cast, I caught a nice trout. We ended up catching a stringer of three big fish, which I gave to Juan. I don't clean fish.

We hiked to a great waterfall, had a nice lunch, and found two new friends in Juan and Carlos. All for one hundred dollars.

To fish a day at one of the high-end camps costs $2,500. Same fish and I had better fellowship. I also climbed a volcano by asking another restaurant owner in another town if they knew anyone who wanted to make a few bucks by taking me to the top of the volcano.

I call this touristing on a budget by staying away from the high-priced tour packages. But more than that, it's called connecting with fellow human beings.

FERRYING THE IRON HORSE

AT PUERTO MONTT, I headed on to the legendary Austral.

Carretera Austral is the name given Chile's Route 7. The highway runs 770 miles from Puerto Montt to Villa O'Higgins in rural Patagonia. Most of it is gravel (and mud) and begins in this area.

It was an unusually wet season when I was

visiting. Chile had experienced a drought for several years and needed the rain. All my gear and I stayed wet... and cold.

I felt sorry for myself until I saw the bicyclists. The bicyclists would attempt to ride between towns, only to find themselves camping on the side of the road. Raining and forty-degrees Fahrenheit. It's a challenge to reach the next town by bicycle when it's seventy kilometers away. That's about fifty miles—or three-hundred fifty wet-dog miles.

I would cruise past them—huddled in a ditch, wet and cold, like a homeless dog waiting for a warm home. One couple I met from France was biking through Chile. We were both renting rooms in the same house. Many houses in small towns have signs in the yard advertising rooms for rent. Included with the room rental are a bed and a hot water shower for around twenty bucks.

This young couple agreed renting the room beat sleeping in a tent. The next day, it rained from sun up to sun down. I often wondered if the French couple actually rode the fifty-mile trek the next day. I didn't bring a tent or camping gear on this trip, only hiking shoes.

Over the course of five days, I crossed the water on three ferries, which connect the Austral. The first ferry was located at Coleta La Arena, the second ferry was located at Hornopiren, and the third ferry at Pillan. The ferry trips lasted between one to four hours. The cost to ride the ferries was minimal and was on a first-come-first-serve basis. So get in line early. Snacks and drinks are served on board.

Everything was fairly organized since it's the only mode of travel in the area. At Hornopiren, I was having lunch at a small cafe and started talking to the owner, who suggested I stay a couple of days. There was a seldom-climbed volcano near the town. So I asked if someone would be available to guide me up the volcano since it required bushwhacking, or making our own way on part of the trail.

Bubba arrived and agreed to guide me up the volcano for $75, including lunch. Bubba picked me up the next day in a small truck that required a push to start up. After getting lost on a trail that's never hiked, we finally found our way to the top and made a day of it.

I last saw Bubba when I gave his truck a push to get started. He left me standing in the town square. *Bubba?...* Was I back in Texas or still in Chile?

The gravel roads were in surprisingly great shape, and the scenery was stunning. I discovered my expensive waterproof bag was not waterproof, so I bought a roll of trash bags, which kept everything dry.

The Iron Horse and I were muddy, and we stayed muddy through all of Chile.

Even though the days were wet and cold, the beauty warmed me like sunlight. I really liked the town of Aisen where I found hot springs. I could've stayed there for a week.

I made some new friends, who cheered me on as I made my way down the Austral and onto Tierra del Fuego. It wouldn't be long, and I'd be turning toward the town of Chile Chico, and then into Argentina.

Patagonia was the wildest and most desolate

country I'd ever visited, but I loved it. The land had a wild, untamed ruggedness, and the people who live in Patagonia want to keep it that way. The locals were friendly, helpful, and the most gracious hosts.

A TIME TO GO

MY TIME IN Chile went by fast, and it was almost time to say goodbye. I spent about three weeks on the Carretera Austral in southern Chile.

As I rode into Chile Chico, located on the border with Argentina, I finally hit real asphalt. Riding on asphalt felt strange after two weeks of riding on gravel and mud. As I hit Argentina, I also hit wind.

It wasn't long before I was missing the rain and the mud.

> **TRAVEL TIP:** Always use at least "dual sport" tires on the gravel roads in Chile. Street tires on your motorcycle won't work. The roads in Chile consist of loose gravel and not much asphalt. I used Continental tires, a personal preference, but there are other good brands also available. In Santiago, I replaced my tires.

The Andes mountain range starts in Peru and reaches 23,000 feet above sea level. For comparison, the highest mountain peaks in Colorado reach about 14,000 feet above sea level.

By the time the Andes mountain range reaches the tip of Chile, they've been reduced to almost sea level. This mountain range, as I discovered, blocks the wind and keeps the rain and cold air in Chile. The Andes run the length of Chile and Argentina.

ALONE ON THE MOUNTAIN

I THOUGHT I'D take a shortcut through the National Forest, a thirty-mile stretch of nothing.

About halfway into the National Forest, I started riding up a hill—almost straight up. As I climbed higher, the road worsened until it wasn't a road, but deep ruts in mud, peppered with large rocks instead. On one side was a forty-foot drop-off, and on the other side, which hugged the mountain, deep ruts.

In quick-decision mode, I chose the mountain-hugging side. I knew I couldn't slow down and had to keep plowing over the rocks and through the ruts. There was no time to lament about the size of my motorcycle or about my abilities as an off-road rider.

The other side of the road, inches from the cliff and the forty-foot drop-off, had a nice trail. Seemed everyone chose to hug the mountain. Always take the road less traveled, right?

I saw an opening and went for it. I rode along for a few yards until my front tire hit a softball-sized rock, and down we went. I was probably going too slow. When I regained my senses, the wheels were pointing uphill, and the motorcycle was on my leg. Luckily, my leg was in the rut, so it wasn't crushed.

After fifteen minutes of wiggling about, I retrieved my leg from under the fallen Iron Horse.

Now, to set the Iron Horse on its wheels.

I hadn't seen a car since I entered the park, but if one was coming from the bottom, they'd have to get a running start. A car couldn't make it, but a big truck might be able to. I had a strap in my bag, but it wasn't a ratchet strap. Always carry a ratchet strap, by the way. There was no way I was going to lift an 800-pound motorcycle uphill.

After two hours of trying to figure out what to do, I decided to hike out. I had just four hours of daylight remaining and about fifteen miles to hike. And I had no intentions of camping on the mountain. Too many things can happen, and none of them good.

I piled rocks in the road on the uphill and downhill side of the Iron Horse—to warn other motorists, and as a kind of memorial. After pausing to survey the surreal burial site, I said goodbye, grabbed my backpack full of important documents, and headed down the road.

Of course, I asked and pleaded for a little providential help.

I hadn't ventured a hundred yards around the bend, and my prayer was answered. Two small children, followed by two families with teenage children, were on the road. It required everyone working together, but we stood the bike up and turned it around. Felipe, Carlos, and their families were lifesavers. All natives of Chile, they had moved to Australia and were home for a visit.

Felipe's wife asked if I'd seen a sign a few miles back that read, "Carretera Cerrada."

"Oh, I thought that was a salad," I replied. Now I

know it means, "Road Closed."

Just before seeing me trimming down the road, Felipe's wife asked him, "Why on earth do you think it's a good idea to hike up this hill?"

Now we know.

I was going to wax poetic about God's providence when Felipe spoke up, "It was to save the dumb gringo who can't read a sign!"

And life goes on... in Chile.

Thirteen

ARGENTINA AND THE END OF THE WORLD

CHILE AND ARGENTINA are like two siblings, linked by proximity and birthright. I suggested they become one country and call it "Chile-tina." No one, in either country, thought this was a good idea.

The Patagonia area encompasses the meandering border of Argentina and Chile, and so does the Pacific Ocean and the Andes mountain range. Native Indians have been roaming both sides of the border for centuries—long before there was a border. The border roughly runs along the top of the Andes. Chile was mainly cold and wet while Argentina was cold, wet, and windy.

The further I rode away from the Andes, the windier it became. The app at windguru.com became my best friend. (Put in the town or country, and you'll receive an hour-by-hour report of wind speed.) Too windy to ride? Go back to bed.

My route threaded back and forth between Chile and Argentina about six times on this trip. Honestly, I lost count.

DIRK WEISIGER

MY LONGEST DAY

ZIGGING BACK INTO Argentina from Chile, I noticed the wind had really picked up. I was making good time, and the Iron Horse was performing well. Our speed was good, so I felt I could make it to El Chalten.

As I sat eating lunch in Gobernador Gregores, I knew I had about three more hours to ride. My map showed forty kilometers on the gravel road.

Maps lie.

Forty kilometers down the sandbox—I mean, *road*—I still had thirty more to travel before I'd hit pavement. The gravel became deep and loose, and the crosswind picked up, gusting at forty miles an hour.

I rode in a six-inch deep rut to keep the motorcycle tracking without crashing into the deep loose rock. The Iron Horse and I leaned into the wind and fought for every mile. In a car, with four wheels, the deep ruts help the vehicle not to slide around in the wind. On two wheels, I was way over my skis.

I knew I couldn't hold on much longer, and as I slowed down, the wind took me where I didn't want to go—like a sailboat with no rudder. I slid down twice that day. Both times, cars showed up to help. My ego wasn't too big to accept all the help I could get.

As I finally hit asphalt and headed for El Chalten, the crosswinds were unrelenting. I was very discouraged and exhausted. Some days on the road are like that. I started the morning feeling good about how far I'd progressed as a rider. I even led three Argentinian riders into Gobernador Gregores. I'd successfully tackled gravel on the Austral route for one full week. I had ridden in all weather—from rain to heat to freezing snow. The wind was the only element that brought me to my humble reality.

Based on my day, I felt like I'd gone back to zero as a rider.

Then, *ping!* A timely text arrived from my friend Ian. He sent a photo of three riders who had just dropped their bikes in the Tierra del Fuego. "Keep your chin up, Mate! You'll be fine. Keep going. You'll feel worse if you throw in the towel."

Life Lesson: Don't quit. Fight one more round. Words to ride by—and live by. No matter how good a rider you are, you can be humbled on this trek. Don't ever think you've beaten the weather or the road. Whenever I reach the end of a long, challenging road, I stop and tip my hat. I survived, but I never felt I've won.

I certainly believe the durability of the BMW brand contributed to the success of my trip. My motorcycle was perfect for some stretches, but if I could make any change, I would try a BMW 650. A lighter motorcycle would provide a little more leverage on the rutted and muddy roads. Many other riders agree.

One rider chose a 250 Yamaha for his ride. After hitting a huge gust of Argentinian wind, he was last seen floating over the Andes.

Yes, I was discouraged, but I wasn't going to quit on my longest day!

DIRK WEISIGER

BARILOCHE—A GERMAN ENCLAVE

I WAS ANXIOUS to arrive in Bariloche, a German expat enclave, with lots of beer and chocolate from Germany. After World War II, thousands of Germans settled in the mountainous regions of Chile and Argentina.

The story goes, many Nazis fled Germany and found a safe haven in South America, particularly around Bariloche. Not many years ago, a former Nazi guard was found still living in the area. Some said he was considered a respected member of the community.

What I found was a slice of Bavaria, or *little Switzerland* as some call it. Two Swiss riders on KLM motorcycles disagreed. "Nothing like Switzerland," they claimed.

For some reason, I felt at home in Bariloche—like I'd been there before. I trekked several trails around the town. I ate the food, drank the beer, and stayed in an old farmhouse owned by Christine, who was very familiar with the city. She told me of a German scientist who used to live in Bariloche and tested atomic fusion around the time of WWII—funded entirely by the Argentinian government. *Verrrry interesting...*

So-called cold fusion was studied then and has been for decades. Theoretically, it's the opposite counterpart to "fission" reactors, commonly used in nuclear power plants. But fusion has remained a mystery. What's happening with this promising technology? Nothing. That's the consensus of the

Argentinians who live in Bariloche, but I left with a curious feeling.

Something tells me I'll be back. Bariloche is located deep in the heart of the Patagonia, where there is good snow skiing in the winter and great outdoor activities in the summer.

I could live in Bariloche. I will return for another visit.

COPAHUE AND THE BATHHOUSE

RIDING ON, THE Iron Horse and I found ourselves on a lonely, windy *ripio*, gravel road, with rain threatening. *Freezing* rain.

I was searching for a bathhouse in the town of Copahue, located near the border with Chile. The road literally stops in Copahue. The town boasts of their healing waters and the mud of the mighty Volcano Copahue.

The town closes during the winter because of too much snow. With the freezing rains in the summer, I can understand why.

Tomorrow, I'd be climbing Volcano Copahue, but today, I was ready to find the town, get settled, and soak in the warm, healing waters. After finding a room in Hotel Termas, and getting the Iron Horse settled in, I set out for a bathhouse.

Folks from all over Argentina and Chile seek the healing water and mud that percolates from the volcano. The locals claim it heals anything that ails you, from arthritis to depression. I just wanted a good soak and massage.

As I entered the bathhouse, the sulfur smell permeated everything. One of the attendants, Migel, spoke English and explained the many treatment options available. The next thing I knew, my naked frame was covered in mud—from head to toe. Only my private parts were spared.

I laid on my stomach thinking, *If they roll me over, I'm outta here, and that windows mine!*

The attendant wrapped me in plastic and left me on the gurney for thirty minutes. When the mud was nicely caked onto my body, they unwrapped me, and I showered off. The only feeling I experienced was clean—but after a long day on the road, maybe feeling clean was a miracle—although I still found bits of mud here and there weeks later.

After my mud wrap came a soak in a wooden tub. Folks in white coats, who claim to be doctors so you'll feel better about the treatments—and the price, I suppose—carefully monitored all procedures.

Before stepping into the hot bath, I was checked over by a doctor, someone in a white coat, before the procedure started. Blood pressure—110 over 80—and the answers to ten other questions were submitted to the person in the white coat. All *no*'s, I might add. The soak was nice and smelled of sulfur, so I expected some good would come from the experience.

After twenty minutes in the tub, I had to lie down for ten minutes before moving on to the one-hour massage. All in all, a lot of quality relaxing for eighty dollars. There were a lot of old folks participating in the treatments, and they all seemed content, but that's pretty much the standard, laid-back attitude of South America.

When I'm old—no, not next year—I mean *really* old, send me to Copahue and the Copahue Termas Bathhouse. Deposit me in the mud bath. *If this is heaven, just leave me there.*

SURVIVING GAS

THE NEXT DAY, I had an interesting climb up Volcano Copahue.

This tour included six of us, plus our guide. Copahue is a live volcano, with a constant release of gas. I questioned the safety of the hike, but all felt the necessary precautions had been taken. By the way, precaution means something different in Argentina.

"You want to stay away from the poisonous wind drift," we were told. "If the wind blows the gas toward the east, we attack from the west."

"What if the wind shifts mid climb?"

No answer. I went anyway.

On the drive to the trailhead, I kept seeing signs stating, "Danger, stay out." I asked my seatmate if we should really be here. She smiled and said Argentinians don't read signs. *Locals don't seem to be concerned about danger, and the wind was moving the gas in the opposite direction*, I assured myself.

The climb up became steep, and one of the participants became petrified of the trail. I found myself motivating her to put one foot in front of the other and to keep her walking pole on her downhill side for balance. We were exposed to loose rock on one side of a mountain, which can be unnerving, even for an experienced hiker.

It was apparent the guide and I were the most experienced hikers in the bunch. I brought up the rear of the procession, and as we neared the top, the smell of gas was very apparent.

The wind had shifted.

Scarves were handed out and quickly put on to shield us from breathing in the toxic gas. Instead of wondering how a piece of cloth could protect our lungs, we trudged on. Curiously, everyone's pace quickened!

The view at the top was a beautiful show of green smoke, billowing out of the volcano. Some countries, like Nicaragua, wouldn't let you near gas like this, but that didn't seem to hold back this group of hikers—and the gringo.

I thought we'd watch the volcano for a minute and head back down. I was wrong. It was *mate* time. Mate—pronounced "MAH-tay"—is a local herbal tea drink, enjoyed each day around three in the afternoon. It's a social tradition in Argentina. When it's mate time, not even gas from a volcano would stop the locals from sipping.

Snacks were passed around, and we sat in the "gas" for thirty minutes. I asked the guide about the side effects of breathing this gas every day.

"Death," he answered, and then smiled. "They don't know for sure," he said. "But we should know in about thirty years."

As we headed down, I taught the other hikers how to "ski" the scree of loose rocks, a combination of sliding and running down the mountain in loose gravel. Ironically, our guide wanted to stop us because of safety issues. *Seriously?*

We ignored him and had a great time.

PATIENCE

I FIGURED OUT the problem with South America. Everyone is too patient.

We (me) and everyone north of Mexico, want everything yesterday. We're impatient. What takes a week in the USA, takes a month in Argentina.

The people are just as intelligent, they are very hard workers, and the countries have great resources. We simply have different cultures.

I was in line at a hotel waiting to check out. In what country, you ask? Trust me—it doesn't matter. Guests are required to get a stamp so the parking guards will release your car or motorcycle. The Iron Horse patiently waited. We stood in line—eight deep—waiting and waiting. Finally, it was my turn.

I checked out of the room, asked for the stamp to unbridle my ride, and was informed the guy with the stamp machine was at lunch.

So, I waited for thirty minutes with all the rest of the drivers and riders. We made the most of our time by meeting new friends and trading stories. Water was being sold to those waiting. It was insane!

I finally walked up to the desk and asked about the stamp guy.

"Jose, you finished with lunch?" the clerk yelled to the back office.

"I can't find the stamp," hollered Jose.

"What?!" I yelled. "You people are killing me!"

The lively conversations stopped, and all stood in silence. I had become the ugly American.

A long minute later, Jose emerged from the back with his bowl of soup. "Hey, what's this?" he said with a surprised grin as he pulled the stamp from the soup bowl.

And life goes on in Argentina. We hurry for nothing.

My two favorite places to visit, where there is nothing to hurry about are El Chalten and El Calafate. My favorite side trip was to the Estancia Nibepo Aike in El Calafate, a real working sheep ranch. Both should be on your to-visit—slowly—list, along with hiking the Perito Moreno glaciers at Argentino Lake outside of El Calafate.

And maybe a mud bath.

TRAPPED IN A MUDSLIDE

MOST SAY UNUSUAL things happen during a full eclipse of the sun. You be the judge.

I'd been in Huinganco for three days, trekking and hanging out with my new friend, Claudia. She is Argentinian and knows the area. We decided to venture out on a day trip to Agua Caliente, a natural hot spring, from Volcano Domuyo.

It was a great drive in her Fiat Adventure mini-truck. The fact I was allowed to drive made it all the better. The forty-mile drive on gravel roads made me glad I was in a small truck and not on the Iron Horse.

The road went through switchbacks, down a steep gorge, and then back up the other side. Many places showed evidence of concerning erosion from the heavy rains.

Being the positive guy I am, I remembered thinking how terrifying it would be if the road would give way. The fall would be a good one hundred feet or more. Sheer disaster. The side of the mountain seemed to be made of mud, and I wondered how road conditions would change in a downpour.

Meanwhile, in *reality-ville*, the landscape was gorgeous in the sunshine and looked like a picture on a postcard. The hot springs were relaxing, and the thermal water was just the right shade of warm. I thought this would be a great place to return to for an overnight stay, but the thunder started and reminded us to head back to Varvarco, the nearest town.

At the bottom of the gorge where the river flowed, it started to rain, hard. There were no cars ahead of us on the road, and it was eerily quiet. I had a gut feeling to get out of there quickly. If the river flooded, we'd be trapped.

All of a sudden, boulders, rocks, water, and mud flowed down the mountain like a waterfall and covered the road. I drove faster.

Claudia began to plead for me to stop, but if we stopped, we'd be trapped—or swept off the road into the river.

On my left was the river, straight ahead was a blur of a mud-streaked windshield, and to my right was a river of mud. Underneath us, the road was covered with mud and rocks. I didn't know how long we could keep going, but I knew we couldn't stop.

In situations like this, there's no time to sit and analyze the situation. You've got to act.

We were finally climbing higher, fighting a tide of mud with each switchback. Thankfully, the mountain didn't give way. After what seemed like an hour, but probably lasted only ten minutes, we reached the top of the gorge where the rain let up, and the road flattened out.

We were okay until we saw the giant *zanja* in front of us, a river of churning mud, engulfing the road, and sweeping away anything in its path. We were trapped! We couldn't go back, and we couldn't go forward. Now was the time for assessing.

We had a tent, and there was a stand of trees uphill, where no mudslide would be able to threaten us. We made a call to get help from the military, which controls the national parks. After fifteen minutes, other cars traveling through the park appeared behind us, and we felt much better about the situation.

A few hours passed, the raging river became a stream. A grader rumbled onto the scene as the military crew cleared out the boulders and molded a new road.

The other locals didn't seem to be concerned. This is a common occurrence when it rains. Around nightfall, we made it back to Varvarco in one piece. I felt God had his hand on us, despite the impending eclipse, which was to occur at nine p.m.

I looked at the watch—it was nine p.m.

Washed-out roads may be a common occurrence

for the locals, but this was one tourist attraction I don't care to see again. If there's no danger, where's the adventure? If there's no absurd waiting for Jose to find the stamp in his soup, where's the funny story?

When you face death, the desire for adventure is best written about. Thank God we can. Lost—but found—in the Patagonia.

DEATH STOLEN FROM THE GRIM REAPER

I'VE SAID ALL along that death is only a second away, at any time, for the Iron Horse and for me. That's why you bond so deeply with your motorcycle. Neither would make it without the other. I've also made no attempt to hide the fact that I pray daily for my safety and for the safety of the motorcycle. I even ask for a ten-second delay from any tight spots—wheels coming off trucks, rock slides, potholes, drivers not seeing me, and from people texting while driving.

> **LIFE TIP:** You always have to have your head on a swivel. Drive defensively and always look twice.

I stopped along the highway for gas at Tolhuin, only one hundred kilometers from Ushuaia. I was anxious to finally arrive in Ushuaia.

As I eased back onto the highway, I noticed a car heading toward me in the turn lane and wanting to turn left. The driver was waiting to see what I was going to do—or so I thought.

I looked behind me and saw no one. Thinking the

driver in the turn lane was waiting for me, I started to ease onto the highway. In the next millisecond, a car whizzed by from behind. It was so close, I could feel the rush of air.

It missed me by inches. I had failed to look twice.

This mistake is where I believe providential help saved my life. There is a time to live and a time to die. It obviously wasn't my time to see my dear sweet mom in heaven. As the car zoomed past, my life actually did flash before my eyes. I'm not kidding.

I pulled over for about thirty minutes to gather myself. I realized how fortunate I had been. The two-second delay of making sure the other cars saw me saved my life. Life and death are just that close.

LIFE TIP: Never be afraid of death, but never be unprepared. Are you prepared?

USHUAIA AND THE END OF THE WORLD

MY RIDE INTO Ushuaia was bittersweet.

The thought of how close I came to not making it hung over me like a rain cloud. I couldn't shake it.

After several hours, the dark thoughts gave way to beholding the beautiful scenery and the realization of my tremendous accomplishment. The negative feelings melted away like newly fallen snow.

Speaking of snow, it was in the forecast and was visible on the peaks ahead. About an hour later, I passed a ski resort. As I saw the sign ahead, "Welcome to Ushuaia," a snowflake hit my cheek and melted, or it might have been a tear.

I made it to the end of the world. One year, one month, and one day. Sixteen thousand miles on two wheels!

All the starts and stops, the good fortune and the bad. The breakdowns and setbacks. My stolen laptop, with all my writings. Lost friendships and new ones.

I left a little naive. I arrived a little wiser.

That night in a local pub, a fellow rider commented. "Well, you know, you're not really at the end of the world unless you go to the National Forest and follow it to the sign where the road ends."

The old me might have called it "close enough." But the new me didn't give this a second thought. The next morning, I was on the road—until I ran out of road.

As I rounded the final bend, there was a row of at least thirteen parked tour buses and a long line of tourists waiting for a picture by the sign. Somehow, I felt a little underwhelmed.

My journey to Ushuaia, the way I chose to do it anyway, was special and rare—and should be reserved for the few. I decided not to wait in line with the masses that'd been dropped there by the air-conditioned buses. I just sat and watched as one tourist after another posed at the sign.

A group of twenty motorcycle riders showed up. I offered to take their picture by the sign. They'd flown into Santiago, rented motorcycles, and rode down. They were impressed with my story. "All the way from Texas? Wow!"

A small crowd gathered as I recapped my journey.

One particular young man from Taiwan marveled.

"I flew in from Taiwan and took a bus to get here for a picture. But you rode from Texas! What on earth possessed you to do it?"

"To get a picture," I said, and we all shared a laugh.

But I've thought about his question a lot, during and after my trip. After a couple days, the true answer hit me.

FOURTEEN

THE BOTTOM OF THE WORLD

I SET OUT from Texas to Tierra del Fuego and the tip of Argentina.

I have now been to all three North American countries—Canada, USA, and Mexico—and all seven Central American countries—Belize, El Salvador, Guatemala, Honduras, Nicaragua, Costa Rica, and Panama.

In South America, I've been to Colombia, Ecuador, Peru, Bolivia, Chile, and Argentina. I've flown into Venezuela since the borders were closed.

An average American can travel well.

For the gringo, life is pretty good if you're a tourist and have a little money. If you stay away from drugs and prostitution, you shouldn't have any problems unless you're simply at the wrong place at the wrong time. The gringo always has a place at the table if you have money to pay, treat all fairly, don't complain, and encourage all that you meet with a smile on your face.

In other words, don't be the ugly American. (This takes practice, believe me.)

It was explained to me in Ecuador that gringo stands for "green go." During a war, some war, the American soldier was asked to leave. Thus the slang term was formed, and it wasn't a friendly one.

South America tends not to like us to refer to ourselves as "Americans." In their view, we're all Americans, some North, some South, some central. "US citizen" is preferable. As a tourist passing through, I've found ninety-five percent of the people are good, five percent are bad, and a minute percentage will kill you.

There are all kinds of opinions are out there about living or retiring in these countries. Everyone's reality is based on personal experience, which forms opinion. Even the best of countries will target you if you have big money—either as a government, by the retail practices of working people, or both. If you live or invest in a foreign country, you will always be on the outside looking in. The gringo always pays more.

So enjoy yourself, and be glad you're able to visit a new place and meet new people.

The United States is still respected. Even if there's jealousy or anger, most want to come to the USA if they can. Those I met who had lived here spoke glowingly about the opportunity to make good money, then come back to the mother country and buy a farm, business, or land. They could come back a "somebody."

Those who are desperately poor in Central and South America are a different case. Their obstacle is not the border, but the people preying on their desire to get into the US—the coyotes. These mobsters steal, rob, and kill. It is a life and death gamble. I heard stories about how easy it is to get across, and then how people lost everything (sometimes their life) trying to get across.

All the countries I visited are socialist at best and ruled by a dictator at worst. Most have a bloody past but are relatively peaceful (except Venezuela at the time of this writing).

Don't let *one* story be *the* story. I could tell one story from a country, and you'd never go there. I could tell a different story, and you'd want to leave tomorrow.

Almost without exception, the people you meet simply want to live in peace and raise their families.

BRIAN'S STORY

THEY SAY OUR biggest job in life is our children.

Our job is done by the time they're thirteen or so. After that, the die is cast. They sink or swim on their own. We parents often beat ourselves up too much—or pat ourselves on the back too much, depending on how they do. The truth is somewhere in the middle.

I got lucky... my kids had a good mother.

My son Brian has always been what I call a "silent leader." In sports, he was always the player you could count on. The one who set up the stars on the team. He always played on winning teams, and I believe that was no coincidence.

In all the endeavors he tried, from skiing to hiking, he always did well. In the Air Force, he's a player/coach, always supporting the team. He likes to be right behind the limelight. He would always handle any hiking trip he tried. He mastered skiing in one trip—water and snow! White water rafting was a breeze with Brian. He even finished one summer selling books for Southwestern! He did say one summer was enough, though.

Texas Hold'em... he always wins!

In the Air Force, he works with the video feed on the Drone program. He is a staff sergeant and trains others. He is always my go-to guy. If I need anything, I would always call on Brian, and he always had the answer.

But I always wondered how he would handle serious adversity. Sometimes life throws you a curve.

About three years ago, Brian was injured playing flag football at the Air Force. He and another guy went up for a pass, and he came down with a gash in his head, which required thirty stitches. Three months later, he collapsed at work. Then he experienced a massive headache—worse than the worst migraine.

He went to the hospital emergency room, but they found no cause. They gave him morphine and sent him home. A pattern started. Each time the morphine wore off, the headaches would return. They tested him for everything they could think of, but all tests were negative.

His mother decided to fly to Virginia and get to the bottom of everything, as only mothers can. In the meantime, Brian was laying on a gurney in a teaching hospital at Langley Air Force Base after yet another episode. A contracted doctor in a crumpled coat, who taught interns, showed up, and after one look at the records, started reprimanding the young doctors.

Brian was rushed to Portsmouth Naval hospital. A neurosurgeon was called, who looked at the charts, and decided emergency surgery was the only option. He called me to explain the procedure in which he would go into Brian's skull and extract the puss pocket with a long needle. If he punctured the *other* side of the sack, the outcome would be one hundred percent mortality.

I went from watching an NFL playoff game to pleading with God for my son's life.

Those are moments that bring about desperation. I asked the doctor about his success rate. "One hundred percent," he said. That was good enough for me.

I was on the next flight to Virginia. We all were relieved once Brian was out of surgery.

The next day, I went to find the teaching doctor in the crumpled coat at the base hospital.

For some reason, no one could put their hands on the records. The hospital was being remodeled and in chaos, and I was leaving the next day. I never found that doctor.

Sometimes angels are sent to direct the order of man. Could it be? Brian is well today and doesn't talk about his ordeal. Most good leaders don't.

I wondered how Brian would handle adversity and found he handled it better than me.

Adventure and adversity will teach you more about life than any textbook, any job, or any television show.

DIRK WEISIGER

THE END OF THE TRAIL IN BUENOS AIRES

AS I RODE into the city of three million, I was ready to barn the Iron Horse and enjoy this place I'd heard so much about. I decided to stay in the Palmara district. A place of nice high-rises, parks, and museums. Outdoor cafes, restaurants, and tree-lined boulevards.

My daughter Laura had decided at the last minute to join me.

Buenos Aires has a great subway system and is easy to get around. We had an absolute blast.

One of our favorite tours was the graveyard tour telling stories of famous people in Argentinian history. Also, you can't see this city without a dinner and tango dancing. We enjoyed it with new friends we'd met.

The evening was a perfect way to end my journey with Laura, my biggest fan, and toast a successful adventure in a city they call the "Paris of South America."

LAURA TRAVELS TO URUGUAY

MY PASSPORT WAS full of stamps. Twenty-seven pages with four to a page and I had one spot left to get back in the U.S. *Next time, I'll order a fifty-two-page passport.*

I was busy making arrangements to ship the Iron Horse back to Texas. I encouraged Laura to venture over to Uruguay on "a one-day scouting trip." (I planned on riding Uruguay, Paraguay, and Brazil on another trip.)

Since the acorn doesn't fall far from the tree, she thought this sounded fun. After handling all the planning herself, she headed for Uruguay early the next morning. After watching her get into the Uber car, I felt more than a bit of angst. She looked back at me and waved. I could tell she was nervous, too.

At five in the afternoon, Laura burst through the door of our hotel room, super-excited and talking a mile a minute! She'd met a couple of women from Australia. ("I'm invited to Australia!" she exclaimed.) She toured the beach in Colonia. She tried to rent a Vespa scooter but was told she didn't have a proper license.

She had coffee and mara luna (sweet croissants) in a quaint cafe. She had found her way by taxi to the ferry launch. Then she took the two-hour ride across from Buenos Aires to Colonia, Uruguay. She found her way back by ferry and then subway. After several dead ends to the day trip, she couldn't have been happier. Another adventure traveler!

I was excited and proud. Laura learned several things from her trip.

It's up to you to make your own adventure. (It's not the same if someone else steals the joy of planning and executing.)

No matter what culture you're from, we are all basically the same. (We're just trying to live day by day. Raise a family, pay the bills, and live in peace.)

And she learned that *learning their language isn't always necessary but is appreciated.* (People are very forgiving and helpful if you'll try your best at their language with a smile on your face.)

DIRK WEISIGER

Sometimes living your own movie is about stepping out in faith—with a little providential help, you'll meet the challenges.

Sometimes the road will lead to what seems like a dead end. Sometimes the road will lead to a lesson you needed to learn. Sometimes it will lead to unexpected joy.

But it will always lead to confidence—confidence that you are in control of your own destiny in this journey we call life.

THE END

THAT NIGHT BACK in Ushuaia, I learned something else about the end of the world. At the port, a ferry takes you to Navarina Island. On the island, the road takes you to Port Williams, Chile. That's the last town you can reach in South America.

From Port Williams, there's a trail that heads south about two miles to a small hill where a Chilean flag flies.

And that's the bottom of the world.

As I climbed the hill, I wondered if I would see beyond the sea to Antarctica. At the flag, there was just another rolling hill. But for me, this was the end of the world. I took a selfie of the Chilean flag and me. I sat and looked beyond the sun as it was setting.

The sight took me back to that ranch so many years ago. Back when I had a lifetime to figure out what was beyond the sun.

I had lived my movie. *My* movie. I had walked my journey. *My* journey. I left tomorrow. *My* tomorrow.

A cool wind blew and pulled me from my deep thoughts. I looked back and was surprised to see two hikers with full packs had reached the flag but were hiking on. No, it couldn't be!

"This is the end of the world," I said.

They laughed and headed down the trail. One yelled back at me, "There's always Antarctica!" The journey continues.

I sat there in silence, looked deep into the red-orange sky, and had a moment of blissful déjà vu.

I remembered my time at the ranch some forty years earlier, as I rode my horse, and wondered, *What's beyond this sunset?*

You see, there's always something beyond the sunset. For each of us, that *something* is different.

As the sky turned dark red, I stood up, tipped my hat to the breaking waves, and headed north toward town.

EPILOGUE

WHERE DO WE go from here? Take action for your dream, your movie, your journey. Action will control fear and propel you forward.

These six steps will help you prep for your movie.

1. **Look inside your passion.** You'll need motivation for your journey. Live your dream. Find your calling. But know the difference between ego and calling. Ego fears not having something. Calling fears not expressing itself. Ego needs anxiety to survive. Calling needs silence to survive. Ego manifests as burnout. Calling manifests as fulfillment. Ego focuses on the result. Calling focuses on the process. Ego wants to preserve itself. Calling wants to impact others.

2. **Take one small step.** Volunteer? Buy a book related to your passion. Find a cause bigger than you. If the cause I discovered (the school in Nicaragua) has found you, then you can help children of Nicaragua who may not have a chance at an education or a way out. (Go to www.DirkSpeaks.com and get involved.)

3. **Look for detours along the way.** As you've seen from my story, the obstacles were the highlights. No GPS will get you lost only to discover you're at a place you'd rather be. In the middle of lost, adventures appear.

4. **Have a garage sale and ditch your excuses.** Minimize your life. Will Rogers said, "Too many people spend money they haven't earned, to buy things they don't want, to impress people they don't like."

5. **Keep taking one more step.** Every step changes you and gets you closer to the destination. And away from your fears. Most fear is imagined. Action overcomes fear. Take heavy action. It starts with the next step. Climbing Kilimanjaro was all about the next step. Stop living in fear—especially fear of death...or fear of life!

6. **Start.** I thought about riding to the bottom of South America for at least two years. You know what you want to do. There are plenty of reasons not to. There is always a reason why.

Leave tomorrow.

(And send me a postcard.)

SUPPORT THE SCHOOL

**Want to sponsor children at the
Colegio Bautista El Calvario school?**

You've already helped support children in Nicaragua
by purchasing this book. Thank you!

A portion of proceeds from this book help sponsor
children at the Colegio Bautista El Calvario school in
Managua, Nicaragua.

If you'd like to make a monthly or one-time donation,
please contact me at www.DirkSpeaks.com

**Want to see more photos and notes about each
chapter?**

Go to www.DirkWeisiger.com/Chapters

ACKNOWLEDGMENTS

To all the wonderful people I've met on my journeys, and have yet to meet, thank you for making this world a beautiful place to wander.

Thank you, Brian and Laura. I'm so proud to watch you live your movies.

Amy, thank you for being a wonderful sister and such a help in life and business. You are the reason I'm able to wander.

To my friend JD Dyess, thank you for the two week crash course through Mexico! And letting me use the Iron Horse.

Jodi Carroll, thanks for the counsel that birthed a journey to help me live my movie.

To my book coach, Mike Loomis, thank you for the direction, inspiration, and encouragement to write this book.

Darden Smith, your creativity as a songwriter has helped me think outside the box and get off the hamster wheel.

Abbey Hansen, your artistic talents in these maps put the long trek in perspective.

Thanks to all my friends, old and new, who followed my trip. Your encouragement kept me going.

And to Dad, Jack, who is the original wanderer and storyteller.

DIRK AND THE IRON HORSE

ABOUT THE AUTHOR

DIRK WEISIGER is a travel trekker, trick roper, and storyteller.

As a teenager, and through years of building a successful business in the insurance industry, Dirk has always enjoyed speaking to groups—spinning tales and ropes.

He's travelled to five continents and climbed Mount Kilimanjaro. Dirk tries to live his own movie, and inspires others to live *their* movie.

Most of all Dirk loves people and believes that making new friends is the best part of travel.

If interested in booking Dirk to speak to your conference or group, please contact us at the web address below.

www.DirkSpeaks.com

For all your long-term care insurance and Medicare supplement needs, go to: www.summitlongtermcare.com